New Haven Ratchet Business

Business

Part 2

by

Stacey Fenner

CONTENTS

Visit Stacey Fenner's Facebook for the latest news and updates.

Instagram: authorstaceyfenner

Twitter: @sfenner1

Facebook: www.facebook.com/authorstaceyfenner

DEDICATION

In honor of my late Mother & Brother

Last year was the worst year of my life. Parts of me left and will never ever be the same again. I'm still trying to wrap my head around the fact that you're both gone. You two were my biggest supporters; I'm so lost, I just pray that I find my way! The only thing left to do is make the two of you proud of me! I'm going to strive to be the best that I can be!

Watch over us like you're our Angels and let the blessings flow! Gone, but never forgotten!

Rest In Peace

Darin Fenner

Aug. 9, 1967- June 27, 2016

Paulette Fenner

Sept. 12, 1946- Dec. 14, 2016

ACKNOWLEDGMENTS

First and foremost I have to give an honor to God, all thanks to him for giving me the gift to write.

To my father and mother, Lester & Paulette Fenner; without them there would be no me.

To my husband, Mr. Keith Blackwell, my rock, my strength, my backbone, my everything. Thank you for being the best husband that I could ever ask for. I love you.

To my two lovely daughters, Jasmine & Janay, my pride and joy. There is no greater honor in this life than a mother that gets to watch her children grow up and become the young women that you are today. I'm so proud of you both. Keep reaching and achieving your goals! There will be many roadblocks that you will have to go through, but continue to push. There is nothing that's impossible!

To my Nook, I love you so much. You give me so much life; your smile alone gives me such a warm, fuzzy feeling inside.

To the rest of my family & friends, I thank you so much for your ongoing support and the love that is shown to me! I love each and every one of you!

To my hometown, New Haven, CT., thank you for all that ratchet business. Please keep them stories coming!

To SWP, aka Sharlene Smith, and the rest of the staff, and to Secretly-Charmed LPromo, thank you for your continued promotion.

To Tiffany Lynne of Gray Publishing Services, thank you for all of your services. I appreciate it from the bottom of my heart!

CHAPTER 1

THE BUM SQUAD

PONCHO

Dealing with these women just got real, my wife and side-chick having an affair. I'm all fucked up behind this shit. Now, I'm the type of dude that can handle a lot, but I'll be damned if I saw this coming. *This explains exactly why Lisa deprives me, and when I'm laying pipe she's like a dead corpse.* Wifey likes that same thing that I like. I wouldn't have a problem with it, but she don't want no dick up inside her. Man, when I walked in the room I thought I hit the jackpot. I was like, 'Well damn, I get to have my wife and side dish all together at one time. Shit let me join in.' I started stripping off my clothes and said, 'Let's go!' Lisa wasn't trying to hear it; she said it ain't that type of party. *Yeah, that's right. It was a party alright, just with no dick in it!*

Talk about a bruised ego, I can't even begin to explain how I'm feeling. For a dude like me this should be heaven. My wife told me that I can do what I want to do, as long as it's not disrespectful to her in the public eye. I can have as many women as I want, except for Honesty, because she's in love with her. All these years I thought that's what I wanted from any woman, now that it's handed to me, I have a problem with it. I just don't understand how she don't want all this pipe I have to offer. A woman can't do what a man does, period. *What the hell they get out of rubbing clits together? WHACK! WHACK! WHACK!* The shortage of men got these women swinging all kind of ways. Sexually all confused and what not.

Now Honesty is the one that got some shit with her. She's mad at me for not telling her that I was married. Mad at my wife for not telling her she had a husband. But she failed to mention that my wife was her reason for moving down here in the first place. Shit is just confusing as fuck! What gets me is that Honesty knew what the deal was when I brought her to the house. She was the one playing games the whole time. Her mama should've named her Liar, she's good at it.

My squad don't even know about this. *How do I even begin to explain this?* They'll be laughing at me for life if they get wind of this. Especially Quan, he'll never let me live this down. I'm going to have to come up with a lie as to why I'm leaving. Staying here ain't doing nothing for me. A little alimony and another bitch to take care of me is the mission I'm on. It might take me a minute, she has to have more than Lisa and love her some dick. *I know she's out here; I just have to find her.* There's a couple of women in the church that I have my eye on, but I'm looking at them wondering if they're the same way Lisa is. Shouting, praising the Lord, and eating pussy…skipping over Sodom and Gomorrah. *One experience was enough for me.*

I been chillin in the house for the last couple of days trying to collect my thoughts, very rare for me. I'm always in the streets. My fake ass wife is trying to avoid me, when issues need to be addressed. Ever since she got caught up she has me sleeping in the basement, but today, before she goes to work, we're gonna have an early morning conversation.

*****

I made my way upstairs to the bedroom where she was getting dressed, walked in and startled her. "Lisa, let me ask you a question. What kind of marriage is this?" I asked.

"A perfect one, for a dog like yourself, and a perfect one for a woman that doesn't like penis. You shouldn't be having such a hard time with this. You can do whatever you want to do…I don't care." Lisa was putting on her clothes. One of her many pantsuits that made her ass look flatter than it really was.

"All of this for the church, why didn't you just stay single?" I walked straight up on her with the need to be right in her face.

"My family and friends have been putting the pressure on me for years. Here I am, so successful, looking like I have it all together with no boyfriend or husband. Everyone wanted to know when I was getting married and having kids. When I ran into you it was perfect. I said, 'Here goes a dog that's looking for a come up. He won't really want me because he's too busy screwing on every corner of New Haven.' It was a perfect idea to get people out of my ear. I needed an out, and you were it. This is a win-win for the both of us." She walked away from me like it was no big deal, grabbing her shoes to put them on.

"Well I think you should just tell them that you're straight up gay. No need in all of this, joke of a marriage. Or better yet, tell them you're a nun." *I don't really appreciate being involved in a scam. Only the ones I create and know about.*

"I come from a religious family, they will never understand my lifestyle. I'm making you look good and you're making me look good. One hand is washing the other, but my dad wants to know when you're getting a job. You might have to get you a little part-time gig so he doesn't think that I'm being taken advantage of by my husband." *She can't be serious right now! Me...work? Her and her daddy got another thing coming. As long as I'm in this, she's going to pay me to keep my mouth shut. Anything I want, I better get.*

"A job? Yo, I'm not getting a job just so you can please daddy! If you were really so concerned, you would open your mind up to men and women, the way God created this Universe to be! Pray to the Lord to fix that mind of yours. All you had to do was let me know from the giddy up!" If Lisa would have been on the up and up then we could have worked something out. I would still have married her, but under these false pretenses…now shit has to be my way. She led me into this blind as a kite.

"You are not a saint, far from it! Just like you never told me about your baby mama that you were living with when we got married. Uh yes, I did my homework. You thought you were marrying a fool." *She's holding in more than I thought. What else does she know that I don't know she knows? This is what I'm talking about. I could still be over there with Chris. I never had to hurt her the way I did.*

"Where do we go from here?" *I know where I'm going, but I need to see what's in her head.*

"Just carry on like we've been doing. I think we make good roommates. You have your little man cave all to yourself, and I have the rest of the house. To God be the glory, we are on the right path." *Lisa has a lot of jokes. Stuck in the basement forever? Is she insane?*

"No, I'm talking about long term. If I can't make love to my wife, what's the sense in having one? My sexual appetite, well let's just put it to you this way, with no disrespect, I like to fuck straight up, no chaser." *Ain't gonna be no small talk. Let's just get down to it.*

"Well, we have something in common. I like to fuck too, just not a man. You can do all the fucking you want to do; it just won't be me! I'm not depriving you, all I'm saying is just try and be discreet. My church members and my family don't need to be coming back to me telling me they saw my husband doing anything other than loving me." *Sho nuff, she has lost it. Lisa has gone crazy.* I never heard her cuss before, always so righteous. *There seems to be a lot that I don't know about her.* I'm expected to keep up with this facade, acting like some happily married couple for her church family!

"Listen here, Lisa, you better start liking dick if you expect me to go along with this charade that you got going on. I have never been in a house with a woman, besides my mom and sisters, that I wasn't fucking. I understand that I'm free to roam in other pussies, but I want yours too. The woman that I married will fuck me or else we are headed to court and I'm taking your deceiving ass all the way to the bank, and to the front of the pulpit!" She got the right one alright, she will be giving me some pussy when and however I want it.

CHAPTER 2

LIZ

All Tyson and Chris had to do was just be honest from the beginning. I wouldn't have been mad if they had just come clean about having a one-night stand. It happened before me, but all the secrecy is what tore me up. Chris, being my girl, could have pulled me up, and Tyson, being my man, could have told me. All is forgiven but there will be no second chances. I made myself very clear to the both of them.

I don't need any reminders of Poncho, or that cruddy ass Dominique. You want to make me bounce, then show me you're like them and you will find yourself on the outside looking in. I'm loyal and dedicated to this relationship and all my friendships. This is the very reason why I haven't had many relationships and don't do so-called friendships.

Instead Tyson called Chris, like he lost his mind, to have her tell me, when he could have just told me himself. All the extras were uncalled for. He was shocked when I answered the phone, 'Oh no you will not play me.' Then Chris called herself coming out the bathroom trying to snatch her phone away from me. *Wasn't happening! I needed to know what was going on.*

I hung up on Tyson ready to swing on Chris. All I could picture in my mind was her blood splattering all over that apartment. I was so heated that a fire extinguisher wouldn't be able to put out my fire. I told her she had sixty seconds to tell me the truth or that was going to be her ass! I wanted every single detail too. I told her, 'Don't leave a damn thing out.' That's when she told me that her and Tyson had a one-time dealing. It wasn't nothing, just some straight up comfort sex for her. *That's why she was acting salty towards me and Tyson's relationship.* She wasn't sure how I was going to react. She was scared she was going to lose me as a friend, and she almost did. It took me a couple of days to calm down and be reasonable with the situation.

I gave Tyson hell. I wasn't speaking to him and was calling around trying to find me another place to live. I didn't want to go back to my place and live with Chris. I was just an emotional mess.

Mika was the one that calmed me down and told me I was going way overboard and acting like they had an affair while we were together. When she put it to me like that, I had to agree, she did have a point. I was overreacting and wanted my relationship with Tyson to work, so I decided to stay and work things out. He kind of got a pass because he wanted to tell me from day one when he found out that I rocked with Chris, she was the one telling him not to. Now Tyson understands that I don't want to hear shit about him that wasn't already told to me by him.

*****

Mika, Mika, Mika. I tried to warn this chick, told her over and over again to leave Rich and his slimy ass alone. Any dude coming out of that Poncho camp ain't about nothing. When she walked in her apartment and found Keisha on her knees sucking on Rich, I would have lost it. Mika would rather stand there, yell and cry, but not me. We would have been thumping on that bitch! Ain't no way. *And she had just took that pregnancy test that came out positive too. Oh Lord, thank God it wasn't me. I still got too much street in me.*

Then Keisha was talking shit to her and put two knots upside her head then left out. Slashed her tires and busted out her windows. I would have been on my best NWA, Fuck tha Police! I'll help defend Mika, but she has to be trying to defend herself first. *I'm not fighting her battles, but I will fight with her.*

Two weeks later Keisha got picked up and arrested again. Wanda told me she's out on bail after sitting in there for thirty days. I hope she stays away from Mika and the baby she's carrying, if not then I will have to involve myself. That's my godchild she's carrying, and not a damn thing better happen to her.

I'm trying to be there as much as I can for her. You would think that I knocked her up as much as I call and check on her. I've been the one going to her doctor appointments, taking off from work, doing my part. I don't want her going by herself. It's her first time going through with a pregnancy, and she hasn't told Rich yet. Matter of fact, she hasn't spoken to him since the day all that drama happened. When she's ready I guess she will tell him. Right now I can't even speak his name. In due time he will find out...once she starts showing. New Haven can't hold water, so the word will get around and land right in his lap. She's only three months, carrying small. I figure around five months she will have a belly. *Speaking of Mika, I need to make my daily call.*

*****

"Hey," Mika answered.

"How are you feeling today?" Morning sickness was kicking Mika's butt.

"Sick as usual, how's work?" Mika had to take a leave of absence. Too sick to work, the doctor put her on bed rest. I have a feeling she won't be returning.

"Work is work, same old stuff. Nothing interesting going on over here." *Extra boring now that she's not here. I have nobody to talk to. All these chicks want to do is gossip about one another.*

"You just had to take that supervisor's position and mess everything up for me. I could be sitting across from you now, chatting it up." Mika tried to laugh, but it was faint. The doctor gave her medicine for her morning sickness. *So much for that.*

"No you couldn't. You're too sick for that. You should be feeling better in a couple of weeks. This has to be a boy. I was never this sick with all three of my girls." *I'm hoping for a boy. Hopefully things go my way.*

"You're right, I would be sitting there gagging all day. I hope so, can't take much more of this. I've been over here considering having an abortion. It wouldn't be so bad if I wasn't sick twenty-four seven. I'm ready to get back to normal." *Come on now, Mika, I asked you if were you sure that this is what you wanted to do and you said yes.* It's her choice. I'm not too fond of her situation, but if God gave you a baby and you go full term, then it was meant to be.

"What's your percentage on getting this abortion? The baby is starting to form now. We go for our first ultrasound next week and that vision will forever be in your head. Maybe we should cancel the appointment until you're for sure." *I hope she changes her mind and just has the baby; maybe I'm being selfish. I was looking forward to being a godparent.*

"I'm like at the halfway mark. I'll let you know by the end of the week how I'm feeling. Love you girl. Call me when you get off. I'm going back to sleep, hopefully." Mika sounded drained. All she does is sleep. *She makes me not want no more. I change my mind. Tyson better be happy with his one and my three.*

"Okay, just text me when you get up. I don't want to interrupt your sleep." I hung up the phone. Maybe me and Chris should go over there one day this week to uplift her spirits.

I was trying to get some work done when I saw that Wanda was calling me at two in the afternoon. Monday through Friday she only calls after five. I didn't second-guess myself when I picked up the phone.

*****

"What's up Wanda?" Whatever it was, it couldn't wait.

"Girl, I told you that Champ was out of jail." Champ is Wanda's man that has been locked up since God knows when. I haven't heard that much from her since he's been home. *Good, because now she had her own business to tend to.*

"Yes I know." *I think the whole world knew the way she be posting his ass all over every social media site.* What I want to know is what does this have to do with her interrupting my workday?

"I need a job, you got that supervisor position! Can you get me in there? You know he's fresh out and ain't nobody trying to hire him!" Wanda was sounding as if her relationship depended on her getting a job. *If Champ is that hard up for money then he should be out there trying to make a dollar, not Wanda.*

"You need experience to work here and all I can do is refer you. I don't have the final say-so as to who gets the job." I don't remember Wanda ever working. How she pays her bills is beyond me. I'm not nosey so I've never even asked. All I know is that she's never asked me for any money, so we cool.

"Things are real tight around here. What kind of experience? I'm pretty good with the computer." *Of course you are, you're only up there all day long.*

"We process insurance claims, do you know how to do that? It's basically data entry. Or you could apply for the customer service position and be on the phone all day." *That would be a good spot for her since she likes running off at the mouth.*

"Oh yeah, I'm going to apply for them both. I need a hook up. My bills have doubled since he been home. I feel like I'm feeding the whole neighborhood. I got a house full every day. Champ has to stop catering to his boys when we're on a budget. I'm starting to get stressed the fuck out, girl. I mean, I'm glad he's home, but damn, we broke all the time. He over here mad at me, telling me that I should have had my shit together as long as he's been gone. For the past week all I hear is, 'Did you find a job yet?' I'm tired of hearing his mouth." *Hmm something don't sound right, but okay. I'll vouch for her, but it ain't going to be on a strong note.*

"Go online and put in your application. I will see what I can do." Wanda would fit right in with the rest of the gossipers. *As long as she don't talk about my business to these folks, we good. What little she knows anyway.*

"Girl, thank you! I'm going up there right now. I'll text you when I'm done so you can go pull some strings." *This is going to be interesting. At least she's resting her mouth these days, dealing with her own problems.*

CHAPTER 3

CHRIS

"Poncho, you been over here every day, claiming to see your son. Are you having marital problems already?" *I knew it wasn't going to work out. Something is brewing, and it ain't good. He's sniffing up my ass again.*

"I can't come see my son? We missed a lot of time together because you were acting stupid." *Who does he think he's fooling? This is not about our baby.*

"Oh, I was acting stupid? Do you really want me to go there? I don't think this is a conversation that you want to have right now." *Don't bring me back to that dark place.* I'm just getting to the point where I can stand to see his face.

"Nah, my days of upsetting you are over. I meant to say, when I was acting like a jackass. I'm going to the mall, is there anything that he needs in particular?" This fool been bringing on the bullshit strong. Dropping off and picking up from daycare, now he's spending money. I'll take it while it lasts, might not ever see this kind of help from him again.

"You can get him a coat, it's getting cold. A size 3T; make sure it's black. Your son likes to dirty up stuff. He can always use some more clothes." I'm probably pushing the pedal a little too hard, but we will see. He's never done anything, so this will be a first.

"Do you know what size the girls wear or should I just call Liz myself?" *I do know, but I'm not telling him. Poncho needs to talk to Liz himself.*

"Not off hand, guess you will have to call her." If his wife is giving him money like this then please stay married to the dummy.

"Alright I'm out. I'm going to take him with me. I'll call you when we are on our way back. See you in a little while." *You're starting to spoil me Poncho, this extra time to myself I can get used to.*

"Okay, see you two later on!" I hope Poncho don't think he's cock blocking because I'm going to do me whether he's in our lives or not.

*****

It's sad to say, but I still love his no-good ass. Poncho has a hold on my heart like no other man ever has. He doesn't have my mind anymore and that's a good thing. My mind knows that he's no good for me, no matter how much I care. Wishing he would change, dreams of us being a happy family, but some people never grow up. All he wants to do is swing dick around. *I really wish I knew what men get out of that. How many women do they need to be satisfied? Mom was right about a couple of things, a dog will always stray. No one woman will ever have his heart, so his wife has another thing coming if she thinks he won't put her through hell.*

I'm trying to move forward, dating other dudes, just for the hell of it. It's something to do instead of lying around here letting my mind wander. Trying to find that special someone that will sweep me off my feet. Had I known that Tyson was about something, I would have played those cards different. Who knew my one-night stand would be the key to Liz's happiness. I sure screwed that up, just like I did with the rest of my life…always settling for a man's side dish when I should be the main course. No more roles unless I'm the leading lady. I won't settle for less this time around. My mother did it very well, and I followed right in her footsteps thinking that it was okay. That was until smoke blew up all in my face. I'm now the victim of what another woman's pain feels like. I've come a long way, but I still have my days and nights where I suffer.

*****

I'm on my way to check out Keisha and see what she's been up to since she's been home. We put aside our differences when I saw her standing at the bus stop in the pouring rain the day after she got out of jail. She was headed to see her probation officer and I gave her a ride. I promised her I would stop by her mom's house since she lost her apartment. Keisha couldn't really fill me in with her side of the story; I was headed to work and didn't want to be late. I'm finally off of that probation that my job had me on, and have no intention of getting back on that hit list again. I can't afford to, don't want to mess Liz up after she put her neck out there for me, subletting her apartment to me.

I pulled up and parked in front of Keisha's mother's house, not thrilled about going in there. It's always been nasty. Don't know how they can live like this. I threw my pocketbook in the trunk; her mom has one of those houses where you don't bring anything in so you don't bring anything out by accident. As soon as I stepped on the porch I could smell the aroma of rotten trash. *Oh Lord, I feel like throwing up. Keisha is going to have to come out here and sit in the car with me. I can't do it.*

*****

"Hey girl, what you standing out here for? Come on in!" Keisha swung open the door before I could even knock. *Just when I was about to go back to the car and blow the damn horn. She must have seen me pull up.*

"Hey," I walked in with some serious hesitation. Looking around, this house made Sanford and Son look like they were living in Beverly Hills. *This was worse than a junkyard. A GPS tracker wouldn't be able to find me in here. Oh my God, that smell.* It smelled like Keisha and her mother were having a funk fest. I have to breathe from out my mouth; my nose can't take this smell. Kind of put you in the mind of some old ass tuna fish mixed in with dog shit! They have one of them ancient floor-model TV's, but the roaches were inside the screen running around messing up the commercials.

"Have a seat," Keisha was trying to clear some space up so I could sit down.

"No, that's alright, I was just coming to pick you up so you could ride to the store with me. I'll meet you in the car. Tell your mom I said hello!" Whew, I hauled ass back to my car. *Betsy, I never been so glad to see you!* I gave my steering wheel a kiss.

Keisha came running out the house in her nightgown, no bra on, bonnet on her head and barefooted. *I can't even take this chick with me to the store, not looking like this.* She jumps in the car. Immediately I spray some Febreeze. "What store we rolling to?" She had the nerve to ask me sounding all chipper.

"We ain't going to no store with you looking like you just woke up! Let's just chill out here." I hope she don't take it the wrong way, but I'm so serious.

"A store ain't nothing special, I can go like this, but since you acting all bougie. It's cold, turn the car on so we can get some heat." *Bitch, I need to breathe turn on the water so you can wash your funky ass.*

"Okay Keisha, it is cold out here." I need my gas for the week, but I cranked the car up anyway.

"Yeah, but like I was telling you, old girl had me locked the fuck up! Now I know I was wrong for being in her place with a restraining order hanging over my head, but Rich should have checked the bitch. Does he not know that I'm the mother of his children? I probably lost them forever with these charges that I'm facing." *Keisha just won't take responsibility. It's not Mika's fault. Rich does play a part in this mess, but his ass wasn't on the line either.*

"You need to get it together; leave Rich and his women alone and get your kids back. Focus all that energy on bettering you. That's what I'm doing; in the end no man is worth it." *Boy did I have to learn...one hard ass lesson for me.*

"Easier said than done. I know you still love Poncho. How are you holding up?" *Keisha must not be listening to me. I just told her how I'm holding up.*

"Just like I said, focusing on me and my son. When I get down I just look at him, so sweet and innocent. I want to raise him to be a responsible young man that respects women. Not to do the stuff his father does." *My son will not follow in his father's footsteps...believe that.*

"I called DCF this morning, I'm trying to get my visits back. This shit just set me back like ten times. Before I got caught by the Po Po I went and tried to mend fences with Dominique, just like I promised Rich." *Well at least Keisha is a little focused on her kids. I know that baby must be getting big.*

"Really? I'm proud of you. That was a big thing to do. How did it go? Did she forgive you?" *Give me all the scoop on this right here. Inquiring minds want to know.*

"Nope, she said she will never forgive me. To tell you the truth, I made things worse. I lied and told her that the kids weren't his and that I made it all up in my head." *What in the hell did she do that for?*

"Keisha, Keisha, Keisha, you just made yourself look like a crazed fool that would do anything for a man. To top if off, you kept saying that you wanted it out in the open. Now you just put it back in the dark." *Just when you think you heard it all.*

"I know. That's what she said, but I needed for her to forgive Rich and let him back in. I wasn't about to watch him be with no other woman. I just did it to please him. Desperate measures, for real. Now I'm like, I shouldn't have done it. Have you seen him?" Keisha was staring out the window.

"No I haven't, I have my own issues with him. Even if I did, I wouldn't speak to him. Don't have nothing to say to him. Smiling to my face but was best man in Poncho's wedding. I'm keeping my distance from all of them niggas." Yep, call it what you want, but Poncho wasn't the only one that did me dirty.

"You can't be mad at Rich, what was he supposed to do? Tell on his boy? He wasn't going to do that. You wouldn't tell on me!" I am a little guilty because I'm damn sure not telling Keisha that Mika is pregnant by Rich. Just minding my business, staying in my lane. Keisha will be back in jail if she knew that, so me keeping my mouth shut is saving her from some more charges. Third time around with the same female…oh Keisha would be doing some time.

"Well I am. He was like a brother to me. Did Dominique even take him back?" Me and Rich were better than that. He's told me things before, about Poncho, that I kept between me and him.

"I'm not sure my family is being very closed mouthed when it comes down to them and that sacred marriage. I haven't seen or heard from him since I pulled that little stunt. He has another thing coming if he thinks I'm going to sit over here quietly without making any noise." *Oh Lord, what is this girl up to now?*

"Leave it alone, Keisha. You will run into him eventually." *She must like jail.*

"Nope, I'll find him. I'm just getting some other things in order. My probation officer told me not to go to near him. That if I do she will lock my black ass up! He won't tell on me. I know he wants some of this good loving." *Thank goodness! Poncho just texted me, they're on their way back from the mall. Keisha needs to go soak that thang in a tub full of bleach before she even thinks about spreading them legs.*

"Alright Keisha, I have to head home and get my baby. Call my phone if you need me." *Wrong thing for me to say. Keisha needs me, and a whole army full of psychiatrists to help her.*

"Okay girl, I'll be in touch. Stop by anytime. I'm normally in the house, bored, or sitting on the porch." *No thank you! I already have to air this car out. Now I can breathe normally.*

CHAPTER 4

THE BUM SQUAD

RICH

*W*henever the weather changes the squad switches up spots. It's getting cold, so we move a block away and meet at the Exxon on Whalley. This way we can sit in the car and talk and not freeze to death standing outside.

I've been out the loop. Finally landed me a job through the temp agency, loading trucks. After I'm there ninety days I might get hired, if they like me. My hours are eight to four, coincides well with Dominique's schedule. She can get her sleep before she goes in, while I take care of the kids. She gets them on the bus and I pick them up from the after school program when I get off. Bring them home and start dinner if she's too tired to cook in the morning. Once I get them settled and help with homework, sometimes it's too late to go out. Just enough time to lay it back down and get ready for the next day.

Our parenting is working out well, but the marriage is still rocky. I sleep in the guest room. Dominique won't even let me touch her...not even a hug. All the shit she was complaining about, I'm now giving her, and it still isn't enough. Giving her money for the bills, helping out more with the kids and the house, working my ass off, even working some Saturday's, plus staying out the streets. *What more can I do?* Today I have some free time so I'm waiting on the crew. Dominique took the kids to the movies. I offered to go, but as usual, it was a no.

✶✶✶✶✶

"What's up man? Where the hell you been, or should I say, who you been in?" I laughed. I haven't been able to catch up with Poncho in the last couple of days. Since we don't get to see each other, we usually hit each other up to make sure we're among the living.

"Nah, nothing like that, I just been chillin in the house." Something's up. If Poncho wasn't sick, he wasn't just sitting in no house.

"Yeah right, not you my man! What's really good?" I pushed my seat all the way back. *Poncho is holding out on me.*

"Seriously, other than chillin with my little man, I been in the house. I get up, bring him to the daycare, pick him up and drop him off to Chris. Changing things up a little bit." *He must be back*

31

messing with my girl Chris again, and don't want to say anything.
What's the big deal? It was just a matter of time.

"Alright, alright, how is Chris doing these days anyway?" I
stumbled on her a few times, but the guilt just kept me away. I tried
to act like I didn't see her; don't really know what to say to old girl.

"She seems to be doing okay. These women kill me. Go
through a breakup, hair be done, clothes be on point, but I couldn't
get that when we were together. Now every time I'm over there she
looking flier than a motherfucker!" *Poncho over here sounding like*
he got a problem with seeing Chris look good, but she never was a
slouch to begin with. I guess he's tired of seeing wifey in a skirt or
dress pants every day, looking like an old maid.

"You know that's how they do, trying to show us men what
we're missing out on. Dominique is the same way. Before, all she
wore was her uniform. Now she comes home, gets some rest, and
changes into clothes. When I come home from work and she
happens to be up that day, man she's looking like a dozen roses and
smelling all good." It's starting to get to me a little bit. She does it
on purpose, but I just play it off like it's all-good. When she walks
out the door I'm swinging punches in the air. I be so pissed off.

"Don't tell me Dominique got you in that house, still begging,
while you paying bills?" *This is why I don't like talking to my boys.*
I'm doing what a man is supposed to be doing; they should try it.
Don't knock me for trying to do the right thing.

"Remember, I'm only there for the kids' sake, according to her.
The more I try, the more she pushes me away. All I can do is hope

that the more I prove myself the more she will realize that I'm on the up and up. I ain't even gettin none. Two days is too long for me. Man, I'm a couple of months overdue in that house; beating my shit, looking at magazines like I'm locked up." I could have kept that to myself, but frustration was starting to build up.

"Damn, you still in the dog house! She's winning and you over there losing out; can't even get a piece of ass! Shitttt, you better go make up with Shorty or find you a ho in your spare time." *Poncho and his one-track mind. There's more to life than banging everything with a split in between the legs.*

"I ain't seen Shorty since that day I got busted, wasn't nothing I could say or do but pack my things and get out of her way. I'm not even going to attempt to try and go back that way." I'm already fighting for my wife, Mika would just be another job, and I don't have that much energy. I fucked up once again with Keisha, and I'm leaving it as is. If I run into her I'll apologize again, but that's the best I can give.

"You really are a changed man, Rich. By now you would have had you a side piece. How's that job coming along, you still loving it?" Poncho asked.

"It's alright, a steady paycheck and no begging for a dollar. I feel good being able to help out and bring something to the table." I was throwing Poncho a hint. *Man, it's time you dig in your own pockets.*

"I hear ya, to each his own. I'm gonna keep on hustling these women; that's job enough for me. Getting paid to bust a nut...nigga

I got the best job in the world. You could be hustling up them dollars like you did back in the day, only this time, instead of drugs, let women be your hustle. I'm telling you man, they will take care of you better than that paycheck you getting. You just have to find the right ones, and they out here deep. Stop trying to be the man, and be the man…you know what I'm saying!" *Naw, I don't want to be a bum all my life. I like having my own money. It may not be much, but it's better than waiting on a woman's paycheck.*

"Yeah, it sounds good, but it comes with a lot of problems. Women are a damn headache, too many of them will cause me to have a heart attack. I'm not as smooth as you, homeboy. You have to have patience and a bunch lies!" Me and Poncho shared a nice laugh on that note.

If Dominique keeps this up I will be back in the streets hoeing it up, getting what I can get out of these women. Call me bitter all you want, but hey, I can say I tried doing things the right way, and if it doesn't get me anywhere, then fuck it. I will just do me and never wife up another woman.

*****

I chilled with Poncho a little while longer before heading home. The rest of squad was a no show; not sure what happened, but we'll probably catch up sometime this weekend. I might even hit up a club, haven't done that in a while. My intentions were to take Dominique out to dinner and a movie, but if she ain't droppin them panties, I might as well go look at some ass.

By the time I got home Dominique and the kids were just settling in. I knew she had to go to work in a couple of hours so it caught me by surprise when she started watching TV, chillin on the couch. My bold ass sat right down next to her.

*****

"How was the movie?" I asked, just making some small talk.

"Well, you know it was for the kids, but it was okay, I guess." Dominique was brushing me off and her body language let me know that she didn't appreciate me sitting next to her.

"What's up? You act like you don't want me near you?" *Let's see if she's woman enough to admit it.*

"I don't. When I look at you all I see is Keisha. Even if she claims those kids don't belong to you, I'm still on the fence about that. Her kids look like our kids, and maybe it's because she's my cousin, but I don't know. Let's leave the kids out of this for a second…you still fucked her! You been there with her dirty stinking ass when you have a very clean wife that held your ass down! I was there each and every time your ass had to do a bid! I took your ass back after you cheated on me several times. Now that you're doing right, the one time in your life, I'm supposed to bow down and be grateful. Well tell me what I get for the millions of times that I was doing right by you and getting fucked over?" *All I wanted was a civil conversation, not to have her huffing and puffing, rehashing the past.*

"I said I was sorry for everything over and over again. Don't act like you always held me down either. When I was getting that money you were very well taken care of. Do you want us to continue on like this or are we going to fix our marriage? Right now I'm in this shit by myself!" Things have to change around here and if she's not willing, then I need to figure out what direction I'm headed in.

"You got some nerve. I've been in the marriage by myself since we got married. All you had was the title with no responsibility. The agreement that we made was for you to be here for the kids, not me! Now you want to be this big, old, happy family. You should have thought about that before you laid down in the dirt of nastiness! Were you thinking about all of this when you were up in Keisha's pussy?" *Poncho is right, I'll never win with Dominique.*

"I'm trying, can I least get some credit for that? Should I just go out here and get me a girl or what? I'm a man with needs. Beating my shit, I only did that when I was in jail. Tell me what you want? Matter of fact, who are you fucking?" How do I know she's holding out? My mother always told me when a woman starts giving you her ass to kiss she has somebody.

"I should not be your concern. We can go back to court and you can pay your child support. Come and get the kids every other weekend and end all of this." *Dominique didn't answer not one damn question that I asked her.*

"You want me to leave then?" Maybe she can be straight up with me.

"I want you to do whatever your heart can handle. I'm giving you a choice; that same choice that you never gave me." *I'm getting nowhere so I just have to do what I need to do.*

CHAPTER 5

LIZ

"*L*iz, I need to talk real bad; need to vent for a minute."

Wanda can't you see I'm eating my lunch. Every day she makes her way in here, don't make me regret getting you this job, and it's only been a week.

"What's wrong now?" Wanda looked like she was about to cry.

"Champ is what's wrong. Girl, he's already got my whole paycheck spent before I even get it. I have bills to pay." *This is not even a conversation that we need to be having. She has gotta be kidding me.*

"Wanda, I feel like we keep talking about the same thing. Your bills come first, then you, then him…if you feel like it. Don't let that nigga come home and start running shit when he ain't bringing in nothing but some problems." *I have no time for stupidity.* She's always talking about somebody else and can't handle her own.

"I'm stressed out. I come home to a house full, even when I go to sleep the house is still full. I cooked last night, enough to last us for two days, and the food was gone when I got up to go to work this morning. He didn't even leave enough for me to take for my lunch. I'm hungry, what you over there munching on?" *Food, what does it look like? The same thing I eat every day at lunchtime.*

This is the third time this week I ended up sharing my lunch with Wanda because she was hungry. "Here Wanda," I grabbed another plate and split my food with her. I just can't see her go hungry, but she better wake up and smell the coffee.

"Oh, thank you! When I get my check this week I'll treat you to lunch." Wanda was tearing up my leftovers from last night. *How is she going to treat me when the check she doesn't have is already spent by Champ?*

"Don't worry about it, just buy you some food to put in the freezer here at work, so that you will have it for lunch, since you can't keep none at home. I hope you know that you're going to have to put Champ out. Send him back home to his Mama. Let her put up with him." *Whew, thank God for Tyson. He would never, ever, do me like this.*

"Good idea, that's exactly what I'm going to do." *I hope she means put him out and not buy the food.*

"So you're going to put him out?" I asked just to be sure.

"I don't want to put him out yet. No, I meant buy the food. I'm going to give him another chance; maybe go home and talk to him." *Okay, well he will continue to run all over her. Talking don't get you nowhere with the type of man she got. You have to show him.*

"You've been talking to him Wanda. It's not sinking in. Listen, friend to friend, you were doing just fine by yourself. Don't let that man knock you down on your ass! All that gossiping that you do, take some of your own advice. Cut your losses and move on, like you used to tell us." Wanda is quick to criticize the next chick and can tell everybody else what they should be doing with their life, but can't apply it to herself. That's how it is though, all the ones running their mouths talking about people behind their backs are full of shit.

"My lunch is over, thanks again for getting me this job and letting me vent in your ear. I just have to figure out what I'm going to do about Champ. I'm going back to work to answer these phones. See ya later." Wanda walked out of my office with a sad face. She had ten more minutes left, but didn't want to hear what I had to say. Now she will go out there talking to them gossip queens like herself, only for them to spread her business all over the workplace and be the laughing stock.

I just want us all to win and be happy. I'm no hater; when my friends are happy, I'm happy for them. No matter what my situation may be every woman deserves to smile and glow. There are good men out here…they just need to be found. For every woman that's complaining there's a man doing the same thing. The good men need to meet up with the good women. *Speaking on good men, let me call mine, I haven't heard from him all day.*

*****

"Hello," Tyson answered. His voice still moves me in a loving way.

"How's your day going? I figured I'd call because I haven't heard from you. No text, no nothing." Tyson always texts or calls me throughout the day.

"I was trying to be funny. It's one sided, sometimes I want you to reach out and check on me." *Awww my baby is feeling some kind of way.*

"You're right, I can do that. Sorry sweetie, I appreciate every part of you. Have I not been showing you how much I love you?" *Tyson is the light of my life; I don't ever want him to feel like he's on the backburner.*

"Well that's better, because you haven't been showing me lately. I appreciate you too, but sometimes I would like to hear and feel it from you. You're too consumed with Mika and this baby, Chris and her messed up dates, and Wanda and her jailbird. When I'm right here being neglected." *Guilty! That's all I've been talking about...my girls and their problems.*

"Communication babe, just tell me and I'll listen. Life gets a little crazy, and I guess I been slipping. I do apologize and I will make it up to you." *This weekend I'm going to find a babysitter for the kids and we're going to get some alone time.*

"Alright, alright, I want to see what you come up with! Men like surprises too. I could use a nice massage. My back is giving me grief." *Aww hell naw, I need that back in tact.*

"What time you getting home? Are you working late?" *I'm going to pick up something to eat, that chicken I took out will have to wait. There are more pressing things at stake here. I'm putting these hands to work.*

"I should be home regular time; around four I guess." *Well, we have a meeting in the bedroom.*

"Okay, I'll pick up some food on the way home and help the kids with homework. You just go get in the bed and rest that back until I'm able to apply my special touch. Dinner in bed for you tonight." *Tonight my man will get pampered.*

"Sounds good to me. Yes ma'am, that's where I'll be waiting for you." *Damn, I love me some of him.*

"Love you. See you soon." I hung up the phone disappointed in myself.

*****

I'm glad that Tyson let me know how he was feeling and didn't hold it in. That's how some men go astray, not getting what they need at home. Next thing you know Sally done slid her way on in there. Going from a dog like Poncho to a good man like Tyson, I have to put my all into him. If I can do it for a man that didn't deserve it, then why should Tyson settle for less from me? The man takes care of me and my daughters; picking up the slack from Poncho, I'll be damned if I'm going to half ass him.

That's the problem with these chicks, they take advantage of a good man; taking him for granted, but will fight for a sorry ass man. Backwards thinking, and I never want to fall in that category.

Poncho called me the other day to get the girls sizes so he could buy them some clothes. I should have let Tyson tell him so he could have felt cheap. He ended up getting them two outfits each, and came by the house to drop off their clothes. I let the girls run out there to get them and thank him. He could have given me that money towards getting their heads done, that's a costly expense. *I better get what I can before that wife of his gets tired and the money train stops.* Instead of me getting a babysitter, maybe the girls can go over to his house this weekend. Tyson's son is going with his mom and it would be nice of Poncho to take his. Let me shoot him over a text.

＊＊＊＊＊

Me: Hey, can the girls come over to your house this weekend? You haven't gotten them in a while. I think it's about time they meet their stepmother.

Deadbeat: I was thinking the same thing; I'll pick them up from school on Friday. You don't even have to pack them a bag. Whatever they need, I'll get it.

Me: Okay, thanks

Deadbeat: Welcome, anytime.

*****

Whew, I like this Poncho. If he keeps up this behavior I might have to take back half of the things I say in my head about him. Good, so now that he's getting the girls, let me get a backup plan, just in case. I don't trust him like that, and it's nothing worse than making plans that I can't follow through on.

CHAPTER 6

CHRIS

This dating thing is just not working out for me. I keep meeting the worst, no matter how I do it. Online or in person, these men are just a mess. I met this dude at the grocery store, named Travis. He said he wanted to take me out; we exchanged numbers and talked on the phone for a few days, getting to know each other. He asked to take me to the Olive Garden for dinner. We get there and he claims he's not hungry, but I am. We sit down at the table and he says he just wanted to watch me eat. His stomach was so-called, 'messed up.' He didn't want to let me down or for me to think that he was standing me up. Okay, it's awkward enough that I'm the only ordering for one, but there are two of us sitting at the table. By the time my food arrived, I guess his stomach had healed. He took a fork and started eating off of my plate. Tacky, tacky,

tacky! He ate most of the food and I went home hungry, making myself a burger to fill my halfway empty stomach. A total, epic fail on his part. He gets no more of my time.

Then I met this dude, Dave, online. We were hitting each other up for a minute, chatting it up. The conversation seemed real, so let's exchange numbers and talk where I can finally put a voice to what I had been imagining he sounded like. His voice was much deeper than I thought. A Barry White sounding dude, with a rasp to his voice. He asked me to meet him at the Elk's Club for a drink. I did, figuring that was cool. At least we would be in a public place. I get there, take a seat at the bar, and he comes from out of nowhere, reeking of weed, cigarettes, and too much to drink. He was drunk, a turnoff for me. He looked like a really handsome dude in his pictures, but I must have been cat-fished, with his no teeth having self and a stomach looking like he needed to be induced into labor. Before I could even think about ordering a drink, I was out. An emergency came up, had to pick up my son unexpectedly.

Now there's Smitty, who never really got a fair shot because I was dealing with Poncho. I ran into him on the way home from work one day. I'm looking and smiling and so is he. The timing is right, so why not. We both know each other from back in the day, let's see what we can rekindle. He's a street nigga, always has been, so I'm going in with my eyes wide open. He tells me meet him in Cross parking lot in thirty minutes, so I do. I'm feeling kinda horny and need him to break me off a little something. He jumps in my car and we call ourselves getting it in, making up for old time sake. All of a sudden he starts spazzing out on me about a roach that he pulled out of his asshole. I was every nasty bitch that there is, I forgot that Keisha left a nest when she got out of my car. I thought I killed them all when I bombed my car...evidently not. I'm trying to explain myself, but Smitty was pissed the hell off. Jumped out the car, butt ass naked, shaking his clothes out, being extra precautious not to get any in his car. I was left lying in my car seat, pants down, and a hot, wet ass pussy that couldn't get fucked. *Damn, Damn, Damn, I give up!*

*****

I tried hanging out, but the clubs and bars be full of a bunch of thirsty women, with about five men having their pick of the crop. The dance floor be filled with a bunch of women on it. *Who in the hell wants to dance with a woman?* I like to dance, but I want to intertwine with a man, swaying to the music. New Haven is just sad when it comes down to dating.

*****

Poncho caught me on the right day. He just happened to be dropping off our son and he was sleeping at the time. Once he laid him down on the bed, I gave him that look like, 'If you don't bring your ass in here and tear these walls apart, nigga, I will fuck you up!' He read every bit of what I was saying without me saying one word. Yep, I gave in to the forbidden fruit, and I loved every bit of it. My insides exploded just from his soft, gentle touch, caressing my body all over. Tongue going in and out of his sweet spot, taking me to ecstasy; then when he got to stroking...*Oh my God the man is gifted.* Flipping me every which way, hitting it from the front, sides, back and pulling me on top of him, riding that pony like I never rode one before. I'm surprised the baby slept through our love making session. The love making noise was so fierce that you would have thought it was thundering and lighting outside. Afterwards Poncho wanted to take a shower. *Oh no, sweetheart. Go home to your wife smelling like me from your mouth and all over your body. She don't get that respect from me.*

Yep I ended up dipping backwards, but I got the monkey off my back, just what I needed. My whole attitude changed and my smile was back. Amazing what a sexual encounter can do. I'm on top of the world. I released so much stress into the atmosphere. I can't tell Liz, she will have a fit. I can hear her mouth now. Damn, she will not understand. Then again, she should. She knows how Poncho flips it up and rubs it down. Tyson was alright, but he wasn't no Poncho, or maybe it's different for her. Every woman isn't the same. Guess it depends on what you like and don't like. What's even crazier is how I had both of her men, and we don't even look alike. Our personalities are different. Liz and I are the total opposites that attract the same type of men.

*****

I told Mika I would stop by and drop her off some soup and crackers. If I ever get pregnant again and it's anything like what she's going through, I'm aborting, straight like that. This baby is kicking her straight up the behind. *How do you lose weight when you are pregnant? She's supposed to be gaining weight. Every time I see her she just keeps getting smaller and smaller.*

We've been spending more time together then me and Liz. She's all tied up doing family things. I can't wait till I have my day to be all booed up with a dude. Single life is a lonely life. I don't care how you try to go around it…we all want to be wifed up. Let me go up here and check on my Toots.

*****

"Hey Toots, how are you feeling?" I used my key to get in. Mika gave me one for emergencies.

"A little better today, thank you." Mika took the soup. "When is this morning sickness going to go away?" *She asked me this same question every day.*

"I don't know, mine wasn't that bad. I think I was sick for the first month then after that I was fine. Did you call the doctor?" *I feel so bad for her.*

"Yes, he's sending over a different kind of medicine for me to try. I hope it works. I been to Yale three times this week from dehydration, getting pumped with fluids." *Yeah, I would have been at the clinic, bye baby, bye.*

"Awwww I wish I could do more for you. Have you thought about telling Rich?" *He did have a heart and might come help her out some days.*

"Fuck him, I don't want to see him nor have anything to do with him. I have to go to court next week with crazy. I'm trying to see if I can get a postponement. The prosecutor hasn't called me back yet. There's no way I can sit in a courtroom all day as sick as I am." *Uh yes, good idea. If Keisha even thinks Liz is pregnant she'll try and rip the baby out of her stomach.*

"Yeah, you can't do that. All you need is a doctor's note. You should be fine." At least I hope, you never know with this system. I'll talk to her about Rich another time; every father deserves to know about their child. Whether he's going to be there or not at least give him the option.

"I'm so sick of life, it's just depressing. Why can't I just be happy for once? My disability check is barely covering the rent. I finally got my food stamps but can't eat anyway. I was already on academic probation from the school. It's going to be hell trying to get back in. Now I have a baby on the way, a job I can't stand, and no damn man. Nothing is going right, nothing!" Mika has one of her crying fits at least once a week. Her emotions be all over the place. *She just needs a little pep talk. I'm getting depressed...shit my life ain't much better, but I need them food stamps up off of her to help me out.*

"Let's just focus on the baby first. You can face those obstacles when the time comes. Stop thinking so much about stuff you can't change right now. Dry up them tears, life will not always be this way. Our days of happiness will come, just imagine all good thoughts." *Liz told me the same thing and it helped me out.*

"Chris, I used to be optimistic, thinking that I'm going through all of this just so that I can recognize Mr. Right whenever he comes along. I've been fooling myself. How many people do you know running around here happy? Compare the happy to the unhappy and see how that equation works out! I'm not talking about the people that are happy for a couple of months or for the moment. I'm talking longevity. I'll wait on your answer!" *I have no comeback. Almost everybody I know is complaining or in the same boat we are. This can't be life!*

CHAPTER 7

THE BUM SQUAD

PONCHO

"*Y*ou think that you can just drive over here, nigga, like you ain't get married? Like I'm supposed to be cool with it." "You and your wife still playin games?" Honesty asked. *I see she still has her ass on her back.* I ran into her yesterday on the Ave., we talked briefly. I asked if I could stop by today.

"What about you playing games? You knew damn well that you were in that same house with me several times. You never said shit, why is that?" *Tell me what's really good.*

"I sure did, then I put one and two together. Y'all both were trying to play me. She was bringing me upstairs and you were bringing me downstairs. She was lying and so were you. Neither one of y'all mentioned husband or wife. You told me you were unattached. I'm single, so I can do who and whatever I choose to do, with no explanations. I don't owe nobody shit." *Okay, she might have me on this one but she still could've said something.*

"Let's skip the madness, when was the last time you saw Lisa?" *I want to know if they call themselves still fucking.*

"Since you caught us, she's been calling and texting but I don't respond. Really I don't have much to say to either of you." *Well why am I here then? I didn't force her to get in this car with me.*

"I hear you, what's the deal with you liking women? You can be straight up with me!" *I'm trying to get some clarification. This is a first for me. All the women that I've encountered, to my knowledge, like dick.*

"I can be straight up with you but you can't with me. Funny how that works. But to answer your question, I like people. A good conversation turns me on, and sexually it's the same result. As long as I have an orgasm, we good." *Honesty must like whatever. I'm still confused. This woman don't know what the hell she likes.*

"Let me ask you like this, do you prefer a man or woman? Penetration or a fake strap-on? Like, what is it? Balls or rubbing clits? Tell me, I'm new to this!" *I hope I worded this right, so maybe she'll own up to the name her mama gave her.*

"I prefer whoever treats me right, that's all that matters to me. Your wife was kind and gentle with me. She really does have a heart of gold. Anything that I asked for, she makes sure I get it. I moved here to be closer to her so she wouldn't be doing a lot of traveling. Once I got here, her time was still limited. That's where you came in the picture. I got lonely. I knew she couldn't commit to me; she's so busy upholding her family wishes." Honesty shrugged her shoulders like it was a disappointment. *I see this as an opportunity.*

"What about us? Could you see yourself committed to me?" I like kicking it with Honesty. She's a cool chick.

"How, when you're married to her?" Honesty looked at me like I was speaking a foreign language.

"The marriage is fake, that's how. She bamboozled me into marrying her so she could look good. Lisa doesn't even want me. She won't even let me touch her. Why do you think I was spending time with you?" *Well it's kinda the truth. I'm going to make this work for me.*

"Oh, she did you the same way! Now I get it, see this is pissing me off! She got you to marry her and me to move to New Haven to be with her at her leisure. She's a mess in herself. I'm sorry she did this to you. I can only imagine how you feel." *Yes, this is going in my favor that's what Lisa gets.*

"Yep, I know I lied to you in the beginning, but she just lied all around. Lisa got us both. You know she had the nerve to tell me that I can do whatever I want to do as long as I do it in a respectful way. What wife tells her husband that it's okay to cheat because she don't want to be touched? I'm divorcing her ass. I can't do this. I want to be married to a woman that wants all of me, not just parts!" *I'm putting on strong for Honesty...only thing is she don't have no money. Who's going to take care of me if I go this route?*

"Wow, you really want a divorce and you're open to getting married again?" *Boom, just like that, I got her back.*

"Yep, next time it's going to be with the right one though. My wife is gonna love her some dick!" Honesty started cracking up, but I'm so serious.

"Well that's nice to know. Most men, once they go through a divorce, the last thing on their mind is another marriage." *Uh yeah, I really ain't losing much. Lisa can't get shit out of me, so I won't be the bitter one. If anything, I need my spousal support.*

"I could see us married in a couple of years, can you?" Just throwing this out there in the air because it sounds good.

"That depends on how you act. Are we making us official now?" *Are you droppin them panties? A nigga is hard as a rock and needs some releasing. I'm ready to get up in something.*

"Is my name Poncho?" *I'm just so awesome, loving how smooth I am.*

"Well I guess I'm off the market now." *Now what have I gotten myself into? I'll say anything to bang that back out. This is how I be getting caught up. Feeling one way just for the moment, but these chicks be taking me a little too serious.*

"Let's get out this car and go on inside. Since your wife don't want to treat you right, I'm more than willing to serve you." Exactly what I wanted to hear. Out the car and into the sweet spot, where I love to be.

*****

Yes I still got it. My ego is in overdrive. Honesty got that good, good. Her sweet spot is the sweetest. She knows how to move them hips. I was almost late picking up my son. I wanted to stay in her wetness, but I'm on good terms with Chris, couldn't mess that up either. *Now all I need is a third candidate, then I'll be all set. My future boo has to have some money. Honesty and Chris they cool and all, but they're broke. Honesty don't even have a job. I'm not sure how she's making it and I'm not asking any questions. The last thing I need is for her to start thinking that I'm going to be taking care of her when I'm being taken care of. I don't know...she might have that in mind now that she thinks she's my girl.*

*****

I told Chris don't cook tonight. I'm taking her and my son out to dinner, courtesy of my wife and these credit cards. I been putting a good dent in them lately. She said something about my spending habits the other day. I just looked at her like she was crazy. I'm the Charge King and she's going to keep these pockets full. My idea of paying her back for this fake ass marriage, no dick liking wife. I might as well enjoy it and get everything I can get before I divorce her ass. After speaking with a lawyer, I need to stay married to her for a year. It should be cut and dry because we have no kids together. I'm going to make her sell the house or buy me out, plus make her pay me every month. *Sounds like a good plan to me, only a couple more months to go before I can begin my freedom.*

*****

"Hey," Chris jumped in the car, looking in the back seat blowing our son a kiss. *Damn, I barely beeped the horn. She must have been looking out the window.*

"Hey," I reached over and gave her a kiss. *It's a good thing I wasn't licking on Honesty, but my dick is sticky as fuck.* I need a shower bad, but I sprayed myself down in my cologne that I keep in the car for times like this.

"Where we going to eat at?" Chris was all excited. We've never been out to eat together. I'm trying to prove to her that I'm a changed man.

"Branford, the Chowder Pot. I heard they have some good food." I was just there last week with Lisa and my in-laws.

"Oh yeah, never been there but a lot of people speak highly of that place. This is nice of you, definitely different, coming from you." *Chris better shut up and just enjoy this moment. Slick talking will make me turn this car around.*

"Real funny, I told you things were going to change between us. You didn't believe me, did you?" *Shit I'm trying, that should be good enough.*

"A lot did change, you have a wife now!" *Get over it, Chris. I'm tired of hearing it.*

"I told you, not for long. We're going to be a family again. I want you to push out some more of my kids." *Not really, but it sounded good. I sure will enjoy trying to make some more though.*

"Not until you put a ring on it. Then I'll have as many babies as you want." *Chris has never said anything about a ring. Now that I married Lisa it's all about a ring and marriage.*

"You're going to get your ring sooner than you think. Come on, let's go eat." We pulled up at the restaurant. *I hope we can change the subject over dinner or this might make it worse.*

CHAPTER 8

LIZ

Well I'm back on the good foot with Tyson. I'll be putting him first from now on. He's my future. I understand that my friends may need me, but his needs come before theirs. I'm learning to juggle my time and fit everybody into my schedule.

*****

Poncho held onto his promise to get the girls for the weekend, so all the kids were gone. I took that Friday off to gather up some things that I needed for our special weekend. *It was time to wine and dine my man for the first time since I moved in with him.*

My plans were to show him a good time like no other woman. I ordered some chocolate covered strawberries and added an island theme to our home. Since I couldn't bring him to the beach and sand, I would imitate as best I could. My decorations put you in the mind of Jamaica, nice and colorful with a fountain of love. Oxtails, curry goat and chicken, rice and peas, steamed veggies, and some hard dough bread. A Caribbean paradise, Tyson's favorite, cooked by the one and only me. I put on nothing but reggae music to enhance the scene that I was creating. With the scenery set, food cooked, and me dressed in an all black negligee, ass out, it was a nice treat for him to come home to. The look on his face was priceless as he walked through the door. Our weekend was epic, one that neither one of us will ever forget. The spark was back and now our relationship was flying high. I'm feeling some kind of special. The last place I wanted to be was back here behind this desk. *If I were smart I would have taken this Monday off.*

✱✱✱✱✱

I got up from my desk to go use the bathroom and who do I run into coming in the door, two hours late? I told Wanda not to be messing up. This place don't play, they will fire her. Her ninety days of probation ain't even up. This is show and prove time. Well she can play if she wants to, that's on her. The closer I'm getting to her, her face don't look right. *Her eyes are all swollen from crying, what did Champ do now?*

✱✱✱✱✱

"What's wrong, Wanda?" She tried to put her head down but I saw enough to know better.

"I'll be okay, Liz, don't really want to talk about it." *I can't let her go sit at that cubicle, those chicks will eat her alive.*

"Wanda, you can't go to that desk like that. Go sit in my office, I'll be in there in a minute. I just have to use the bathroom real quick." I watched as Wanda walked into my office shutting the door behind her. *Thank God she listened.* After using the bathroom I made my way back to my office. "Girl, you look like a train wreck. Here, take these shades and tell everybody you have pink eye."

"I know. I'm a mess!" Wanda started crying her eyes out as she took the shades. "Champ did me in this weekend, girl. I came home Friday and he had cleaned up the house; everything was nice and neat. His boys weren't there for a change and I was so happy. It was getting tough going home. I dreaded walking into a full house every damn day. I felt like he was actually listening to me for once." I had to give her a moment to gain her composure because I couldn't make out the rest of what she was saying, just bits and pieces.

"Wanda, I can't understand what you're trying to say, stay with me. Calm down, sweetie." I went over to her so she could cry on my shoulders, just holding her in my arms. Even though I didn't understand fully what was going on, I felt for her." Okay, so I got the first part, tell me what happened?"

"He asked me did I cash my check yet? I said yes, but the bills come first. He wanted a hundred dollars, so like a dumb ass I gave it to him. He was grinning from ear to ear. It's been a long time since he had that type of money on him. Girl, he leaves for the whole weekend, told me he was going down to the corner store. I didn't see him until late last night. I was so heated, I thought maybe he got shot or locked back up. Nigga had me calling the jails and the hospital!" *I hope there's more to this story. Another bum ass has an associate of mine, crying like somebody died.*

"Is he gone, did you put him the hell out?" *All I want to hear is that he's gone. Bye-bye, Champ, and stay gone please. I never thought I would say this, but I like the gossip Wanda better than the crying one.*

"At first he came with this story about how he was sorry and was just hanging out with the dudes since I didn't want them in the house no more. He wasn't going to do it no more, could I forgive him? I said okay, but if you do it again that's it! I wake up this morning to a picture that was sent to my phone of him and some chick, both of them lying in the bed, butt ass naked! With a caption that read, 'Do you know where your man was this weekend?'" *Oh shit!* I almost fell out my chair! *These females is bold as a fluorescent shirt. Just downright disrespectful.*

"Wait a minute, who is she? He just came home not too long ago, where did she come from?" *How does a man that did ten plus years come out of jail and have a side piece?*

"Evidently she's been around for the last two years, going up to the jail to see him. He was getting letters from her on a regular. I found that out after doing some digging. Her name is Honesty Livingston, a chick from Bridgeport that he met through one of the other inmates. It's a wrap. He had to go! Then he tried to lie and say it wasn't him. I'm not crying because he cheated, I'm crying because I can't take back all the years I wasted waiting on him. Can you imagine not getting no dick for almost eleven years because I was being faithful to a nigga that wasn't even worthy? Liz, I can get almost everything back, but time and a dead body!" *Ummmm, I got nothing. Anything that comes out my mouth would be words that would be a danger to society. Now I need a minute to get my thoughts together.*

*****

Wanda was still rambling on while all I saw was a nigga being burned up in flames. You can't even get you a man that's locked up; even they are cheating behind bars. This is past rachet behavior. I can't even call it. I felt so bad for her that I talked to her supervisor for her. She needed the rest of the day off to recover. I really wanted to say the rest of the year. All them years being faithful and he comes home with a side chick after he been living off of her. Wanda was taking care of Champ the whole time he was locked down. Sending him money every month, driving to see him and taking his phone calls. She put her whole life on hold for him, only to find out that there's really no future with him. I could be more understanding if it was a couple of months, but my God, we're talking over a decade. It's very possible to be happily married in all that time. *I need a nice distraction from Wanda and her disaster, let me call and check on my unborn godchild.*

*****

Mika's doing a little bit better with her morning sickness. The medicine that she's taking now is helping her out a lot. She's able to do things on her own now.

"Hey god-mommy, how are you?" *Yes, Mika is sounding like herself and not so dreary these days.*

"I'm good, how's my baby doing?" I can't wait for me and Tyson to have a part in raising this baby. I'm anxious to see how he's going to do with an infant. He didn't always have custody of his son; he didn't actually get him until he was five.

"Oh the baby is fine, kicking the mess out of me. Are you coming to my doctor's appointment next week? We're going to find out what I'm having!" *I'm going to be there with bells on. How dare she insult me like this?*

"You know damn well I'm not missing it. I have it marked on my calendar. I'm taking an early lunch and will meet you there. Don't even try to play me like that!" Mika knows I'm a woman of my word; I'm there every step of the way. I'm already planning the baby shower.

"You know, you've been all booed up lately. Speaking of that, how was the weekend? Did everything go as planned?" One thing about my girl, she never throws shade when it comes down to me and my relationship with Tyson. Sometimes I think she's happier than me.

"Mika, Mika, Mika, it was all of that and then some. I really blew his mind. He was so surprised when he walked through that door. His mouth dropped while he stood there for a moment, girl.

We had a really good time locked in the house with no kids. I didn't even want to come in here today." *Just that quick I almost forgot about my spectacular weekend. I'm glad Mika brought it back to my remembrance. That mess with Wanda had me vexed.*

"Yes, that's what's up! I'm glad you two were able to enjoy some alone time. How did the girls make out with Poncho?" *Oh my, some more madness to deal with.*

"Well they didn't get to spend much time with their step-mother but they did spend a lot of time with Chris. Now ain't that something to be buzzing in your ears. Lately every time I call her she's either rushing me off the phone or I get no answer. Now I know what's up with that. As long as she's okay, I'm good. Her life, her choice, what can I do?" Yeah, this was the highlight when the girls came home, and if Chris doesn't say anything to me about it then I'm just going to play dumb. I'm good at letting people not know what I already know.

"Awwww damn, she went back there! I'm pissed. I hope you don't plan on picking her up again when she falls! I don't even want to hear it no more. I'll tell you what you won't get, this call about me ever dealing with Rich again." Mika was more pissed off than me. *Now she gets to feel what I go through with her. The pot is really calling the kettle black, only difference between the two is Mika moves on to another bum and Chris backslides with the same one.*

"I'm not mad, just don't blow me off like I'm nothing to you now! She can keep it real with me, all I can do is voice my opinion."

I learned a long time ago that people are going to do what they want to do no matter what you say. It's not my burden to carry. Just be the friend that you need to be. You never know what kind of situation any us might get it in.

"Well I am. How you gonna go from being the main chick to the side chick? That's dumb as hell and it's stupid. She's over here coaching me about Rich and his fuck ups. I don't like hypocrites. If she's going to talk that talk then be about that talk. That's like these holier than thou people running around here telling us how we ain't living right, then you catch Mr. Simmons, Ms. Sandra's husband, coming out the back door!" *I caught Mika on the wrong day. A sister is going in.* Years of love doesn't disappear overnight, I don't care how much a person hurts you. *Mika is passing judgment when she shouldn't be.*

"Okay, next topic. When are you going to tell Rich that he has a baby on the way?" *Let's just get back to the Mika business.*

"Never, ever, ever! Me nor this baby want to see him, he violated me!" *The baby is not here yet, or old enough to make a decision like this.*

"Mika, every man that has a child out here deserves to know. Now whatever he chooses to do after he has the information will be on him. Rich will find out that you have a baby and if he can count, which I think he can, he will figure this out. I'm not a fan of his, never have been, but right is right and wrong is wrong. He did violate you, but not this baby, please learn how to separate the two." I'm not going to tell Mika that what she's doing is okay, it's not.

My loyalty is to her so I have to stand by what she says as a friend. At the end of the day this baby is hers and it's not my place to interfere, but I will, by all means, let her know how I feel.

"Say what you want, but that man does not need to know that he fathered my child. I don't want my son or daughter all fucked up behind him! If he ever even thinks that he's the father, I'm telling him I went to the sperm bank, straight like that!" *All I can do is hope that she changes her mind.*

"Girl, don't be upsetting the baby. Calm your nerves down. Go drink you some hot tea and chill out, everything seems to be pissing you off! That's them pregnancy hormones going all out of whack! I will call and check on you tomorrow!" *Whew, that damn Mika gets under my skin some days. She's being so unreasonable. Raising a child isn't as easy as us mothers might make it look.*

CHAPTER 9

CHRIS

𝒪'm getting more out of Poncho now than I ever did. *I'm enjoying this changed man. Maybe him getting married really did work out in my favor.* He finally realized that the grass isn't greener on the other side. For all the pain that he caused me he sure was making up for it. Some would say that he's kissing my ass, but it's the love that he now has for our son and me. Poncho spends more time over here with us then he does at home with his wicked wife. *I hope she knows that a divorce is coming. He never loved her anyway. All she is a meal ticket.* Little did she know, she was paying all my bills, shopping sprees, and dinner was on her once a week. Her credit card even fixed my car, thank you, Lisa. I even have a few dollars in the bank, trying to stay ahead of the game before the well runs dry.

Poncho did explain to me how he got married for us, tired of being broke and not bringing nothing to the table. He should have sat me down and explained it all to me, not let me find out from the streets. I may have still been hurt but I would have understood in due time. When he gets his divorce alimony it should help out, but it won't be like it is now. If he gets the house we can sell it, move and get something more affordable, and pocket the rest. My dreams are finally coming true and I'm starting to build trust again for him. He claims he's done with all the cheating, that I'm enough for him. I never thought I would see a day when he could keep his dick in his pants, but he's showing me; proving me and everybody else wrong.

All that shit my mother was talking to me when I was down and out. *Wait until she gets wind of this. Let's see what the word will be now.* Nothing he does will ever be good enough in her eyes anyway. I'm not taking it personal, she feels that way about every man.

We still haven't made up, I been keeping my distance, as promised. She called last week asking for her grandson, trying to put me on this guilt trip talking about she missed him. My son don't need to go around her or my sisters and hear them bad mouth me. I realize he's still young, but kids can sense bad vibes. My other half of me, Mr. Poncho, thought I was overreacting. His tune would be different if he really knew how my mother felt about him. I started to tell him, however I decided it wouldn't be such a good idea. Once words leave out the mouth, they can't be taken back and I'm not sure how Poncho would take it. Especially with us making future plans, marriage included, and me wanting to have my family in attendance

"I'm trying. Rich stopped by the other day. I knew he couldn't stay away for too long. I wasn't even looking for him, he just popped up over here begging, girl." Keisha was chewing in my ear. *Whatever she's eating it must be real good to her.*

"Mmhmm, so what happened with that?" *I wish I could say that Keisha was lying, but she always tells the truth. Poncho told me that Rich is back with Dominique, still doing the same shit I see. Whew this is going to be one hot ass winter.*

"You know the usual. He got what he wanted. I asked him did he need me to teach his bitches how to satisfy him so he can stop playing with me? He gonna fuck around and I'm going to be gone right in the next nigga's arms forreal. Here I am catching charges behind him, birthed three kids that I have to make a supervised appointment to see. Man listen, he's treading on thin ice. Good thing I'm taking my meds or else his ass would have been fried by now!" *What, what, even Keisha is getting tired of Rich! I wasn't ready for this. Feeling like I'm going to pass out!*

"Sounds like somebody ain't all in love no more! You're doing the right thing. Just concentrate on getting your kids back." *I want to ask her what kind of medication she's on. She's talking like a normal human being for once.*

"Nope, not like I was. I really wanted to bite his dick off and call the cops on him for coming near me. That would have got that restraining order up off of me, discredit his case. But I showed him some mercy." *Who is the woman? Where the hell is Keisha at?*

"Okay, I just wanted to check in and see what you been up to." *I'm tired of her chewing in my ear. That's so rude. Hang up the phone first, then call me back or something. Don't nobody want to hear all that smacking.*

"Not so quick, what's up with you?" I want to tell Keisha about me and Poncho but I can't just yet. I'll wait until we get closer to this wedding.

"Nothing, same old same. I been chilling, ain't nothing going on in New Haven, especially in the cold." Yep, when it gets cold here it's like a desert. As soon as a little bit of heat comes, people come out of hibernation. We get to see what people been doing all winter, stomachs be popping out from whoever got knocked up, cuffing season over, and relationships go sour.

"Ain't that the truth, it's dead as shit out here. My first paycheck girl, we getting on the train and going to the city, you down?" *Only if Poncho let's me. He might start acting funny about what I do and where I go.*

"We'll see. First get the job!" I laughed as I hung up the phone.

I hope Keisha does get the job, this way she can pay for her own dress. Another worry that I had in my mind that I can scratch off the list. Between the two, she should get at least one. You never know what my finances will be looking like by then. I'm willing to pay for the accessories and maybe the shoes. Poncho needs to hurry up and get this divorce done and over with so I can set a date.

CHAPTER 10

THE BUM SQUAD

RICH

"Yo, my man Rich, what's up?" Quan said giving me dap, all happy to see me.

"It ain't nothin, same old same. Trying to keep my head above water. What's up with you?" It's been a long minute since I was able to catch up with Quan.

"I left Tisha's fat ass alone, got me a new Boo! Got me a Molly now, from North Haven. She's white but cool as shit." I was getting ready to ask him who's Camry he was driving, no need now.

"What happened between you and Tish? She got them lights cut off again!" I chuckled. *Quan and his relationships be funny.*

"This time it was the gas, no hot water for me to wash my ass! We in there boiling water putting it in the bathroom sink so we could wash up. Man listen, after a couple of days of that shit, I started re-thinking some things. I was already talking to shawty on the low anyway. Once she took me to her place and I jumped in that hot ass shower it was a wrap. I need stable cable, heat, hot water, and lights! I'm sick and tired of living on the edge, always worried about what's going to be off when I come in the house. I just couldn't do it no more!" *Quan is crazy. He needs a job so he can help keep them utilities on, instead of mooching, blaming Tisha when he's partially to blame. He's in there helping run up the bills, but can't contribute nothing but some food stamps. I can talk now since I have a steady paycheck coming in.*

"Does Molly know what she just got herself into?" *Quan better be careful, Molly just might throw his ass out. Every woman ain't Tisha, and might not put up with his nothing having self.*

"Yeah, we real cool. She has a good heart. She understands that it's hard out here for us black men. Molly is heavy into them politics, she's been reading up on some stuff to get some laws changed." *Laws changed? That ain't why Quan isn't working. He's not working because he's not trying. Quan don't have no police record. I can only imagine the lies he told her. Yep, she's going to get tired of him.*

Just as I was getting ready to dig in Quan's ass. Tisha came screeching up in her homegirl's car, mad as hell. As soon as she jumped out I was like, 'Oh shit, it's about to be on!'

*****

"You sorry ass motherfucker bitch ass nigga! Call yourself leaving me without saying one word to me!" *I was cold, but I'll stand here while it's heating up out here.* We were chillin at the gas station and it was kind of crowded, nobody was going anywhere, all eyes in our direction. Tisha was causing a scene out here.

"Fuck you! I told you that last time that it was the last time. I'm not half ass washing my ass! Pay the fucking bills and you wouldn't have this problem!" Quan snapped back. *This is getting good.*

"No, fuck you, Mr. Cum too quick! Whoever she is, ain't getting shit but a broke, limp dick that can barely get up!" *Damn, Quan having problems with his manhood?* I'm trying to keep a straight face on for my boy, but I had to turn my back to the crowd that was building up by the second to get that fake cough off, but I was really laughing.

"Ain't nothing wrong with me, it's you! Wipe your ass so I won't have to see that dried up shit stuck in your asshole when I'm trying to hit it! You better get the fuck out of here and go back home to your cold water!" *Shots being fired every which way.* The squad was lining up. Mickey pulled up, shortly after came Trey and now Poncho. *Oh we really about to have some fun.*

"Oh now you want to try and talk about the asshole you be licking, nigga go have several seats! Mr. ain't got a dollar, ladies he got you the first of the month with them food stamps though! Let me not forget to give you something you left behind!" Tisha went back to the car and grabbed something out of it. "Here, I know you

76

ain't sleeping too good without your teddy bear!" She threw Quan a stuffed animal, got in the car and pulled off.

*****

"Yo, what just happened here?" Poncho asked with his arms thrown up straight in the air.

I couldn't respond. I was laughing so hard that I had tears coming out my eyes. When I looked around, all the spectators were laughing too. Quan had the teddy bear in his right hand holding onto it. *This is one for the books. That will go down in squad history. I'm glad it ain't me. Let any one of them bring up Keisha again and I will surely remind them of Tisha. Thank you, Quan, you have topped me, my man!*

"Yo, I'm going to walk down the street and get us a drink, something heavy and strong for our man Quan. Who's car we meeting in tonight?" Trey asked.

"We'll be waiting for you in that Beamer. It's that's kind of night!" I said as we all hopped in Poncho's car. "Start this bitch up so we can get some heat!" My hands and feet were cold from standing outside. Quan looked like he was embarrassed, while me and the rest of the squad was still getting our laugh on. He even hesitated getting in the car.

*****

Trey came back with a fifth of Henny, five white plastic cups for all of us and no chaser. This was a straight-up kind of night, so

we could get drunk and vent. *Shittt, we all had women problems.*
Trey had his girl, Quetta's cousin, that came up from South Carolina
to visit, accusing him of getting her pregnant. He would be able to
claim that it wasn't his if he hadn't raw dogged old cuz to begin
with. *Women are scandalous.* He said Quetta went to work one day
and he was sleeping in the bed when cuz hopped on in while he was
sleeping, rubbing on his nuts. His dick got hard when he rolled over
and realized that it wasn't Quetta. It kind of caught him off guard,
but he just went for it. I feel for him. I personally know all about
dipping with the cousin. He should have learned from me and threw
the Ho out the bed, but a man's weakness will always be that third
head. If you give it to us, we're going take it. She don't even have
to be our preference. All it takes is that clit between the legs.

China was pregnant by Mickey and he was trying to convince
her of having an abortion. He already had three kids that he wasn't
taking care of, and hasn't seen probably since they were born, if that.
I know I've never met his kids and he doesn't even talk about them.
All I know is they're by three different females that he randomly
fucked with. China already has five with five different baby
daddies; make it six if she has this one. Mickey is the type of dude
that as long as he's with you, then you and your kids are fine. The
minute they break up he's gone in the wind. He will block it out like
the relationship never happened, and like he was never there for
them kids. No type of attachment. *I wish I could just detach myself
like that.* Mickey is already plotting an escape plan if China keeps
this baby. I know it's some backwards ass shit. As long as the kids

don't belong to him, he doesn't feel obligated, but the minute they do he finds an out. He's a clear version of a man running from responsibility.

Poncho came clean and let the squad know that he has been dealing with Chris again, which we already knew. Sometimes on my way home from work I would go that way and I would always see his car parked out front. At first I thought it was Liz until Poncho told me that Chris moved in and Liz moved out with her boyfriend. *Must be nice to be in a situation where two of his baby mama's get along so well; where they look out for one another.* Then he also told us that him and wifey ain't been seeing eye to eye on some things. We're dudes, so none of the squad got all up in the business, but we all saw this coming. He's talking about getting a divorce in less than a year. *Glad we didn't spend no money on that wedding.* Again, none of us were surprised at all. We knew it wouldn't last for too long. Then he started talking about Honesty like she would be the one for him, if she had money. Lisa had money and she still wasn't enough. Poncho be so full of shit. Whatever woman is serving him right is the one, until he digs into the next hole.

I had to fill the squad in on the no happenings between me and Dominique. I'm a man that made some mistakes; that tried to do everything to please her. My hands weren't doing the job anymore. I needed to feel some flesh and juices flowing. I got drunk and slid by to see Keisha to get my needs served. At first she tried to give me a hard time, but that didn't last for too long. She was easy pussy and I was feindin for her strong head game. I was scared to bust up in her raw, so once I got to that point I pulled out and nutted all over her. I felt better, so did my balls and hands. The squad laughed at me. It was all good. Trey was like, 'Anybody but her,' he called me a fool. *Like he had room to talk.* I just ignored him. Keisha was trying to get her life right. We talked for a long time.

I made it up in my mind that if she doesn't get the kids back then I will take them. DCF has no reason not to release them to me. Poncho is right, let them help me get a place, daycare, food stamps, whatever I can get, I'll take. I'm not living with Dominique as her roommate. If we can't cohabitate as husband and wife, then I don't want it. I'm done trying; I really don't even give a fuck! If I'm married living single then I might as well get it in like a single man.

CHAPTER 11

LIZ

*T*oday is the day that we find out the gender of the baby. I'm all hyped, ready to start shopping. Seems like we been sitting forever. *Guess I'll be late getting back to work.*

"I wish she would hurry up! These doctors kill me, taking their time, but if I was late then I have to reschedule." *Mika ain't never lying, it's the truth.*

"Yep, you right! I'm just as anxious. I feel like I'm having a baby. Tyson just texted me, he wants to know too." I laughed. "Hey have you heard from Chris?"

"Yeah, the bitch been calling but I haven't answered! She's wrapped up in Poncho's world so let her stay there!" *Mika is being so unfair towards Chris, but I'll let it ride.*

"When I text her she responds, but when I call no answer. I really don't care about her and Poncho, so why is she treating me like this? She can call you but not me? That's a low blow." *I'm the one that introduced Chris to Mika in the first place. I thought we were supposed to be girls.*

"Now you see why I haven't answered her. She's full of shit and shouldn't be doing you like this. The same way she can pick up the phone and call me is the same way she can call you. Chris was creeping with Poncho on you and you forgave her, washed it all away, and she turns around and gives you her ass to kiss! Who was there for her when Poncho had her ass crying every night? Now that they are rubbing skin to skin, she forgot all about you. I have no words for her!" *Lord, when is this baby coming? Mika has been on one. It's not really her issue, it's mine and I will deal with it when the time comes. But one thing that I can never question is her loyalty to me.*

"I think you should talk to her and find out what she has to say. Let her know how you feel, no sense in holding it bottled up inside. Maybe if she hears it from another perspective she'll think about it." We never know what's going through Chris's mind. If Mika hears her side of the story she might not be so mad at her.

"Yeah, maybe." Just as Mika said that, she got called in for her ultrasound.

*****

Good news, it's a boy! I'm so happy. The baby measurements were fine and he seemed to be healthy. I was a little worried because Mika is carrying him so little. All my babies were big, but you couldn't really tell that she was even pregnant. She's all baby. I get to play a major role with a little boy after being stuck with three girls. If they would have said it was girl I might have passed out. In four months Tyson and I will be welcoming our godson. When I texted him he sent back a thumbs up, he wanted a boy also. Talking about there's already too many women in the house as is. Even though he has a boy, I'll be able to help raise one from the beginning. *I can't wait to tell the girls when I get home. They always wanted a little brother.* This will make our family complete. Tyson and I don't have one of our own together and I think I need to close up shop. *I'll discuss it with him later.* I'm content with the one's that we do have, and I'm looking forward to them growing up and getting out the house.

*****

I spent most of the day at the doctor's office with Mika and needed to catch up on some work, but I walked over in the customer service department to check and see how Wanda was making out. She wasn't herself and who could blame her. I startled her when I walked up behind her.

*****

"Hey," she said. Putting her finger up for me to wait while she finished up a call. I looked around and all eyes were on me and her. *These chicks need to go back to answering these phones and mind their damn business. So, nosey that it's sickening. I hate walking over here. Most of these bitches can't stand me anyway. The feeling is mutual.*

"How's everything?" I asked whispering. *Don't want to be overheard.*

"Let me take my fifteen minute break." Wanda logged out as we walked back into my office.

"I just wanted to check in with you. Any news?" The last time I talked to Wanda she was supposed to be hooking up with that chick Honesty. Me personally, I wouldn't. A picture says a thousands words, how much more do you have to know? I guess she needed some kind of closure.

"Yeah, I met her in the Stop and Shop parking lot on Dixwell. She don't even have a car or a job. Both of them will be broke together." Wanda should have waxed that ass for sending that pic. A phone call would have been better if she really wanted to put it out there.

"Why didn't she approach you with this the minute she found out about you?" That's what I would have done; set the stage from the moment I even thought I was being played.

"He was playing her too, selling a bunch of lies. He told her that he was living with his mother. Girl, I guess I was the mother. She was even in my house while I was at work on more than one occasion. I remember one of the days that she was talking about because I always make up my bed before I leave the house, and I came home to an unmade bed. Champ claimed he went back to sleep, now he's always up at the crack of dawn. He's still on that jailbird shit. He never goes back to sleep. I thought that was strange but didn't read too much into it. I let it go and went on about my business. Then another time I came home and smelled a woman's perfume, but Champ claimed that Carl, one of his boys, woman stopped by to see what was going on. She thought that Carl was with some chick over here. I let that ride also. Sounded believable because Carl acts like he don't know how to go home. Come to find out Champ was getting money sent to him from me and her. I'm not sure where she was getting it from but maybe she had a job or something. The weekends that I didn't make a visit she was up there visiting him. It's just so much. She gave me an earful." *Why did Wanda invite more pain in her life? If it's over, then it's over. No need in finding out anything else.*

"I bet there is a lot more to tell…a whole two years worth! How did she find out about you?" Out of all the chicks that Poncho was creepin with, the one thing I never heard about was another chick being in my bed. Thank God, he spared me of that drama. All I'm picturing right now is Wanda jumping in that bed and sleeping on some unclean sheets that contain cum from another woman. That's some disgusting ass shit!

"His phone. Champ has two phones. His mother got him one and was paying the bill, but I never knew about that phone. The one

I gave him was a minute phone. The phone started buzzing off when he was out on the porch, so she picked it up and saw pictures of me and him. When she started questioning him about me he told her that I was some chick trying to get with him since he been home. She didn't believe him, and jotted down my number for future reference. You know how us females do. Then she started putting one and two together. She wanted to know what the problem was with him staying over her place sometimes. He would stop by for a little while and leave with an excuse. She couldn't get in touch with him half the time and girl, Champ told her that his mother don't allow him to have female company. That's why he has to sneak her in when she's at work. Then she saw us going in the house together one day when I went to the grocery store. The same so-called chick that she saw in the phone, so she called him on his shit and invited him over to her house for the weekend that he disappeared. She said if it wasn't nothing then I wouldn't respond to the picture that she sent me, but if it was then I would." *This Honesty chick is something else, very messy.*

"You mean to tell me she didn't see any pictures of you when she came over to your house?" *I'm a female; we always scope a man's living quarters for that very same reason.*

"I don't have any pictures up of me. The only ones I have up are for decoration." *I have all kinds of pictures up, even before I moved in with Tyson. I made sure my pictures were all around his house.*

"Oh, well that explains it, these men are something else. You blink an eye and you just might miss something. They are grimy, trifling, and cruddy all at the same damn time! Who got time to be babysitting twenty-four hours a day, seven days a week? That's the only way they can be halfway trusted. The older they get, the more they want to play, it's the total opposite from women. The older we get, the more we just want to settle down and close up shop. These men will leave us with a bad taste in our mouths. Then they have the nerve to say we're bitter when they do the shit they do!" Wanda has me all in my feelings.

"He called and asked me could he come back home, he's sorry. I hung up straight in his face. I have so much less aggravation. My house is nice and peaceful, full of food, and the headaches are gone. Every time I get lonely, I think about all that I would have to put up with. Homegirl actually did me a favor without even knowing it." Wanda is a much stronger woman than me. I know me, I would be up under the jail. I had to go upside Poncho's head quite a few times.

"Just keep thinking like that and you'll be okay. Go buy you a dartboard. When I would get angry I would throw the darts. It kept me out of jail and saved some lives. I don't smoke or drink like that, so it was a technique that I used to calm me." Shoot, I still use it to this day. Let Tyson or one of the kids piss me off, I'm throwing my darts.

"Nah, I'll just stick with my coffee. Let me get back to work, break is over." Wanda laughed at me. *She's laughing now but as*

87

the days go by and them lonely nights sink in…eleven years wasted waiting on a dream; being led on with empty promises. Yes, sweetie, you're going to need more than just some coffee. This is just the beginning of what's to come.

CHAPTER 12

CHRIS

"Poncho, I saw you with a girl in your car and it wasn't your wife! I told you about playing games with me!" He's lucky I couldn't catch up to him; it was like a high-speed chase going down the Post Road. I wasn't letting up, but the cops caught up to me and gave me a hefty speeding ticket. They almost locked me up.

"Baby, listen to me, yes, I was giving that chick a ride home, that's all. I need for you to trust me. When I'm out here in these streets I could care less about these other women! All I want is you and our son! Everything I'm doing is for us, for our future! As long as it took for me to get you back, do you really think that I would take the risk? I didn't realize how much I really loved you until I lost you! That was enough for me!" *Maybe I am letting my insecurities get the best of me. I never heard Poncho talk like this. I have to believe him.*

"Then why didn't you pull over? You started speeding!" *He better make sense and take all doubt away from me. He will not do this to me again. I told him no cheating at all, first signs of it that I was out.*

"I should have, and I should have answered my phone, but you be so irate. I can't talk to you when you're mad like that. Plus, I didn't want you putting your hands on an innocent female that asked me for a ride." *Well, he does know me cause I was gonna put my foot to that ass.*

"I really do want to trust you, but it's just so hard after everything that I've been through with you!" *Now my weak side was coming out, I couldn't help but to cry.*

"Come here, baby." Poncho pulled me to him and wrapped me in his arms, rocking back and forth, kissing me on my head. "I don't know what it's going to take for you to trust me. My days of messing with these other hoes is over. I don't want to live in this world if you're not in my world. I messed up in the past, but I'm building a future with you and only you. I don't want to make you cry again, ever. I want to make you smile. It's me and you forever, but without trust we have nothing. You can't be flying off the handle when you hear or see something! We have a lot of haters and people are going to try and tear us down. I need for you to be stronger than them and know that your man is not out to hurt you, not this time, Chris!" *Awww, he's right. I have to get it together and recognize what's in front of me. He's pouring his whole heart out to me.*

"Okay, I'm sorry, Boo. I promise to do better and just trust that what you say to me is the truth. From this day forward, I'm letting go of the past and I will not accuse you of doing me wrong." *I really made an ass out myself today chasing him down, could have killed myself dodging in and out of cars.*

"Thank you, that's all I wanted to hear you say!" Poncho lifted up my face to his, looked me straight in my eyes and gently kissed me on the lips, sliding his tongue in my mouth to meet mine. *A simple kiss from him has me dripping wet.*

"Now can you please go pick up our son, and drive careful?" He asked as he grabbed my butt cheeks.

"Keep touching me like that and I won't be going anywhere. Matter of fact, my mother can wait. Let's get it in real quick!" *I'm ready to suck and lick every inch of him.*

"Nope, I don't want to rush! I'm going to take my time, giving you them long strokes tonight. I'm gonna tear that sweet spot up until it can't take no more! I want the whole block to hear you hollering! Every position that I can possibly put you in, you will be in. When you go to work tomorrow your whole body will be aching with my name all over you! I'm gonna suck you dry and then wet it up again so you can feel every inch of me gliding in you." *I'm drenched. Um Boo, I need for you to handle me now, and I do mean right now.*

"Please, just give me a little bit to hold me over while I take this ride across town." *I'm ready to jump out of these clothes real quick.*

"Nope, giving you something to think about to make your ride home a little less stressful! I'm going to make a quick run, then I'll be back, butt ass naked waiting for you in the bed. You're on duty to rock the baby to sleep tonight. Once he's sleeping get ready for me to beat it up and have them hips ready to move in motion." *He's teasing me now. My panties are soaked. Poncho has all my juices flowing.*

"Damn baby, but I need to feel you now!" *I figure it wouldn't hurt for me to do a little bit of twerking up on him.* Poncho grabbed me, turned me around, picked me straight up, putting one leg up around each shoulder and started licking my clit with my jeans on. "Oh, Oh, OOOOh, Uh, Uh, OOOh baby, OOOh baby! Oh I like that. Yes, yes, yes!" Just like that, I had an orgasm. That's how horny he had me from running his mouth. It didn't even take much. "Whew, thank you, baby. Now I can go!" Poncho put me down.

"That's it? That's all you needed me to do?" I laughed, giving Poncho one of my many seductive looks.

"That's it for now. I still need you to handle all that business when I get back!" *The party's just getting started.* I grabbed my keys, feeling enlightened, and gave Poncho a kiss between his legs, rubbing his balls. *Oh he wants to play, game on!* I walked out the door going backwards, looking at my cucumber standing rock hard.

*****

The whole ride to my mother's house all I thought about was Poncho. My future husband, having more of his babies, and how happy Poncho has made me. *I damn sure deserved it after hanging in there all them years. Playing second to Liz, then becoming his main, then to being his mistress, now on the way to being his wife. Prayer does work. I prayed that this day would come. Thank you, Lord. Thank you for changing his mind and heart towards me. Poncho is the man I need him to be and he's all mine! Nothing but joy flowing all through me! I have never been this happy in my life.*

*****

I'm in good spirits and I really don't want to walk in here, but I haven't seen my mother or sisters in a minute. I'll go in and speak, and head the hell out of there. She's lucky I let her pick him up from daycare. I was hesitant about doing that. We've been doing just fine without them. I rang the doorbell and my sister opened the door for me. *I see Mom has a new living room set. Must have came from someone's husband. I wonder who he is. Nope, going to continue to mind my business.* Jordan ran straight up to me. "Mommy, mommy!" Jumping straight into my arms.

"Hey there, my little man. You missed me?" I asked.

"No, I missed daddy! He didn't pick me up, Mommy, Gamma did!" *Yes son, sock it to your grandmother and aunts.*

"I know. Grandma missed you. Didn't you miss her?" I was hoping he would say no.

"Yes, I missed my Gamma!" *Wrong answer son.*

"Are you ready to go home?" *Please be ready. No time to be drilled about Poncho. The smile on my face at the mention of his name will tell it all.*

"No, I'm eating Mommy! I have to finish my din, din!" *Great, I thought they would have ate by now. Mom has dinner done by five every day, like clockwork, even on the weekends.*

"Okay, well go in the kitchen and finish up so I can get you home to your bed." Yes, Jordan, your ass better go to bed on time tonight. Mommy has an itch and daddy is going to scratch the hell out of it! I sat down in the living room waiting for Jordan to finish his food so I just picked up Ebony magazine to look busy.

"So you're back with the dog, and moved in with Liz, huh? Exactly what are the three of you doing over there, taking turns as to what bed he jumps in, or having threesomes? Which one is it?" *Only my mother would ask me some stupid shit like this.*

"Mother, exactly where are you getting your info from? You're all the way wrong!" I never looked up from the magazine I was pretending to be reading.

"My grandson, he speaks very well, and he told me that the two of you moved in Aunty Liz's place and that daddy brings him to and from daycare. That sometimes daddy stays late, and you wake him up at night because you're over there crying. From the noises he was imitating, the two of you are in the room fucking, but he talks as if you're upset!" *Damn, Jordan, I'm going to get down to the bottom of this. Was my son volunteering information or was he being questioned?*

"Not that I have to explain myself, but I will get a few things straight. Liz and her girls live with her fiancé. I just took over her lease." I have no excuse for the noises I make, but I have to calm it down some. Jordan doesn't need to be hearing me at night.

"You set a few things straight, but what about those noises? Listen, I knew it was only a matter of time before you started digging back in the dog pound, but my grandson will not be subject to your sexual escapades!" *She's acting as if I'm sleeping with just anybody. Poncho is Jordan's father. That is how he got here in the first place.*

"I was subject to all of your sexual escapades, went to school tired most mornings. So if that's what I'm doing to my son, then I owe him an apology and an understanding that Mommy is not crying; that I'm simply enjoying myself with his father. Not just any man off the street. That's the mess that I had to deal with!" *My mother may have shots, but I got bombs for that ass. Now shut the hell up!*

"Are you talking about the men that put money in your pocket, kept a roof over your nappy head, lights, gas, cable, and phone? The type of men that you never had, those men?" *It's not going to work today, mother. I'm on the biggest cloud that even my eyes can't see.*

"Oh they did all of that, what was that for? To make up for the father that's missing from out of my life? Is he somebody's husband?" *Yes, now mom is pissed. Maybe she will tell me that I'm not welcomed anymore, do me the pleasure!*

"Let me tell you something…"

"Mommy, I'm finished. I'm ready to go home!" Jordan saved the bell. I grabbed his coat and put it on him.

"Tell Grannie bye, bye." I smiled.

"Bye, bye, Gamma! See ya later!" Jordan said bopping out the door. I turned around and looked at my mother as I was shutting the door. She rolled her eyes at me.

As I strapped Jordan in his carseat I thought to myself, *This would be a nice time to have a nice little conversation with him on the ride home. I was always told to teach them young and what goes on in our house must stay in our house.*

CHAPTER 13

THE BUM SQUAD

RICH

"*W*here you been?" Dominique caught me by surprise. *I thought she was at work. I left the kids in the house sleeping.*

"I just ran out real fast! What are you doing home from work?" *Please let the kids be okay. Well the house wasn't burning down and everything looked to be okay so I should be fine.*

"Real fast? I've been sitting here for two hours waiting for you to come home!" *Shit, I'm busted. Then again, no I'm not. As long as the kids are okay why is she questioning me?*

"Are the kids okay?" *Yeah, I'm throwing the ball right back in my court.*

"Yes, they're fine, no thanks to you! Who knows how long you were gone before I got in here? Where were you?" *Who in the hell does she think she is? She ain't been acting like a wife since God knows when.*

"Out. I handled mine, did homework with the kids, made sure they had their baths, ate, and put them to bed." *We roommates, don't be asking me no questions. I do what I want to do.*

"Oh, you being real cocky right now! So, how often do you leave these kids in the house by themselves at night?" *Lately it's been three to four times a week, but I won't tell her that.*

"Why, what is it now Dominique?" *Just say what you got to say so we can move on from here.*

"Your car was seen parked around the corner from Keisha's house. You've been back over there creepin with her! Just go be with that bitch. I'm not even mad. You're just so pathetic! You keep running up in that dirty ass pussy, then think I'm supposed to open up my legs to you? Hell no!" *Here we go again.*

"Why you keeping tabs on me all of a sudden? What, your little work boyfriend ain't keeping you busy? I hope you didn't think that you was going to be out here fucking while I was at home backed the fuck up! Not too long ago you was coming home, getting dressed, and running out talking about you making errands!" *Don't try and kid the bullshitter.* Dominique ain't no saint, either.

"Don't put this off on me. If I'm doing any dirt it's well deserved dirt! I've been the one sitting back taking all your shit that you've dish out on me for many years! I'll tell you this; it's not none of your homeboys, your brother, or any family member of yours! Now, if I did you the way you did me then we might be even,

but I still have a lot of catching up to do compared to you!"
Dominique, you don't want this, nor are you ready! Go take your ass to bed. I have work in the morning.

"Is that all? I have to get up in a couple of hours to go to work, remember?" *As tired as I am, I might just call in. I haven't taken a day off since I been there.*

"Not here. You won't lay your dirty ass in none of these beds! Get your shit and get the hell out! Now!" *She can't throw me out, we're married.*

"I'm not going anywhere, I paid my bills for the month. This is a joint venture, right here!" I pointed all around the house.

"Okay, you stay here then and watch what you get! My man is tired of running in second place. I will not have you messing up my relationship." *Okay this conversation is done. She took it too far.*

"You don't have no damn relationship! We are married! Do you understand me?" I grabbed Dominique by the throat. She must have thought she was talking to her little boy toy. "Come again, what's that shit you talking? You think you gonna have another nigga living in here, up around my fucking kids? Bitch, you have lost your fucking mind!"

"Get your hands off of me! You can run around here and do what the fuck you want, but I can't?" I jacked that ass up in the air. "Put me down, Rich! Now!" Dominique starting kicking and screaming like I was killing her.

"You ain't nothing but a slutty ass bitch! Going around here, trying to make a fool out of me. I know that you work with that nigga! He's going to see me sooner than later, Ho!" *Ain't no woman carrying my last name allowed to fuck another nigga and be blunt about it. She should have let that be her best-kept secret.* "I'm going to fuck both of y'all up!"

"Who you callin a bitch and a Ho? You slime bucket ass bum, mad because another nigga is dicking me down! After you done spread your dick around all over New Haven! It's lovely too, feels sooooo good when he's inside me!" *BOOM!* Punched her dead in the mouth, knocked a tooth out. *BOOM!* Punched her again, knocking another tooth out. If it wasn't for the kids crying, 'Daddy, stop it,' I probably would have killed her.

THIRTY HOURS-FIFTEEN MINUTES LATER

PONCHO TO MY RESCUE

"Yo, get in here man! What the fuck happened?" I made that call to my man, Poncho, and he came through for me. Back out on these bricks, don't know for how long. I'm still hotter than a firecracker. The whole time I'm in there all I could think about was this nigga moving into my house.

"Thanks man. You were the only one that I knew had it to bail me out." Poncho used his wife's credit card to pay the bondsman. My bail was set at twenty g's. Now I'm charged with endangerment to a minor and assault in the second degree, with a restraining order. I don't know when I'm going to be able to see my kids.

"Welcome man, just thank the wife next time you see her. Spill it, I need an explanation." *I don't really want to get all into it...my adrenalin is still pumping.*

"Her mouth got real reckless and I lost control. You know I'm not a woman beater; I don't put my hands on a female. She took me there. She should have stayed at work. Coming home trying to catch me out there, when she been out there! The shit that flashed through my head was me getting up every day going to work, and giving her most of my paycheck for bills. Taking care of my kids, cooking when I have to do, cleaning, and she's out here laying up with the next dude. Then she had the nerve to tell me that he's her boyfriend and I can't be in the house! What kind of shit is that?" *Just talking about it makes me want to go find Dominique so she can catch another five knuckles.*

"Man, you let your emotions get the best of you. Real talk, if you ever want to get back at a woman, it's not with your hands. The strongest weapon you have, besides your dick, is your mouth. All you had to do was make Keisha out to be the prettiest woman alive with the best pussy that you ever had, and admit to her that those really are your kids. Those words would have fucked her up so bad that she would have been trying to kill you!" *Yep, that would have done it, but I'm not through with Dominique yet. I still have time to do exactly that.*

"Yep, and as soon as she puts in for that child support again, I'm quitting this job. She ain't getting shit from me! I'm not taking care of her and no damn man! A woman can't do what a man does.

She's a straight up Ho in my eyes. Fuck her! Expecting me to continue to sit there and beat my dick. If you ain't droppin them panties then you should already know a man is gonna get his!" *She must have forgot who she married. I ain't no fool or piss boy.*

"I hear you. Well, guess we'll both be sitting in divorce court." Poncho laughed but I didn't find shit funny. *I got married to be married forever. It wasn't about what Dominique could do for me. I actually loved my wife.*

"What's going on with you? Bring me to Rob's house, I can't deal with the squad today. I need to clear my head and get in the shower." Poncho was headed to the Ave, and I didn't want to go there.

"Okay, I know how that is." Poncho made a U-turn in the middle of Sherman Ave. "It ain't nothin man. I was chillin with Honesty the other day, Chris was coming home early and saw a female through my tints. It was crazy. She started trying to chase me down. The more I sped up, the more she did. Honesty wanted to know who was that. I had to tell her it was one of my crazy baby mamas that was trying to catch up to me about some money. I told Chris that she needed to trust me and a whole bunch of other yip yap! I gots to be more careful. Both of them think we're getting married. Then wifey zapped out on me when them credit card bills rolled in. I told her that I have eleven kids, what did she expect? Now I just racked up another two thousand getting your ass out!" *Shitttt, I want to be just like Poncho when I grow up, a wife and two fiancée's at the same damn time. This is a nice little distraction from the mess I'm in.*

"All these women can kiss my ass, I'm going to be just like you. Paid and laid. I'm hurt. The minute I try to fly right, this is what I get! My effort meant nothing to her, man! It's all good, I'll never do that again." *The only thing a woman can do for me is spread her legs, use her mouth, and run me some dollars. No more relationship status for me.*

"I been telling you to come to church with me and start there. All the paid women are up in there. Single, just waiting to feel the touch of a man." *Poncho is crazy. I always turn him down because I wouldn't feel comfortable going up in the Lord's house with the wrong intentions.*

"You don't be feeling like the Lord is going to come down and strike you dead? Man, that's foul." *Poncho is trying to have me in hell faster than I want to be.*

"Foul is what we do. That's why you over there hurting! You better hop on this bandwagon! Now get out my car and go cry to Rob, I'm headed to the squad." *Aww shit, I'm going to be the topic of the discussion.*

"Thanks again man, I appreciate you coming to my rescue." I gave my man a hug and hopped out the car. *Now I have to talk to an officer about meeting me at the house to get my stuff since I can't be within 300 feet of Dominique.*

*****

After talking and explaining myself to Rob he took his sweet ass time getting me over there to get my belongings. Then once we got there we had to wait on the officer to arrive before I could go in. My hooptie that I purchased was still sitting in the same place, intact. Dominique's car wasn't there, letting me know that she wasn't home. *Hopefully this officer will let me use my key and I can make it quick. I hate this house now. She can have it. She will never hear me say I want her back again. It's over.* The worst thing you can do to a man is cheat. Before I wasn't sure, just guessing at it, but to hear her say it was on another level. She rubbed that shit all in my face like it was no big deal. *Good, I could see the officer pulling up.*

*****

"Hey, are you Rich?" I nodded my head. "I'm Officer McNeil, I will be escorting you in. You can only take what belongs to you. I just got off the phone with your wife. We gave her a heads up and she didn't want to be here when you came. You can use your key and I will come in while you gather up your things. How long do you think it will take you?" *Hmm, she didn't want to be here. Good, bitch, cause I don't want to see you anyway. I would end up catching another charge.*

"Not long, officer. I just need to get my stuff from out of the room." I unlocked the door and walked in, Officer McNeil trailing behind me.

"Well, I'll just stay down here and give you your privacy. Might check in from time to time to see about your progress." *This officer was pretty cool, almost as if he felt sorry for me.*

"Okay, thanks! I grabbed two big trash bags from out of the kitchen. Dominique hadn't cleaned up the mess we made. I could still see the blood stains on the carpet. I ran upstairs and looked around my room. It didn't look like she touched any of my stuff. *Good for her. That would have just set me off again.* I put as much as I could in both bags and went in each of my kids' rooms. I took one last look around before heading down the stairs. *This will be the last time I ever enter this house. Even when the smoke blows over it will be nothing more than a toot of a horn to pick up the kids.*

"That was fast, you sure you have everything?" Officer McNeil asked.

"Yes, I have everything I want. Whatever is left behind she have it or throw it out." I said.

"Well okay then, if you need to get back in within the next couple of days, just give me a call. I'll escort you again, and listen man, it ain't worth it. Keep your head up!" Officer McNeil handed me his card. "Oh I forgot, can I have your key?"

"Sure, here you go." I gladly gave him the key. "Thank you. You're one of the good ones." I walked over to my hooptie, signaled to Rob so that he could go back home, put my bags in the back seat and pulled off.

CHAPTER 14

LIZ

"Oh what did I do to deserve this phone call?" Chris finally returned my many calls that went unanswered. The girls have been asking for her and Jordan.

"I know, I'm sorry. I've been so busy getting things in order. How are you?" *Yeah right, busy running behind Poncho.*

"That's still not a good enough excuse, but it's nice to hear your voice. I'm fine, how is Jordan?" *I'm just keeping it real. A friend don't act like her. Mika keeps in touch with me. If I don't hear from her, I call and it's vice versa.*

"He's good. My mother finally saw him the other day. I'll tell you about that. What are you doing on this crispy, cold Saturday?" *Cold, just like she's been to me.*

"I'm just doing some house cleaning. Tyson had to work, the girls are cleaning their room, and TJ had football practice. Matter of fact, they told me they saw you and got to spend some time the last time Poncho had them." *Now what you got?*

"Oh yeah, we had a good time together. Can I come over for a minute? I'm not that far from you and I have something I need to talk to you about." *Well this is woman of her. She's going to tell me about Poncho to my face.*

"Sure, I'll listen out for the door." Chris must have been right around the corner. As soon as I used the bathroom and walked down the stairs, she was ringing the bell. I was surprised to see her by herself and not with Jordan. "Come on in." *Chris was hugging me for dear life. I didn't know it was that serious or that I meant that much to her.*

"You just don't know how much I missed you!" *Now I will throw some shade.*

"I can't tell, seeing how long it's been. I was dismissed from your life, not missed. When I miss a person I answer my phone or go and check on them. I don't avoid them at all. I kept trying to figure out was it something that I did?" My circle is small for a reason, I don't do fake. I'm not like the rest; people use the word friend lightly. Since I'm a rare breed, I expect the same in return.

"Can I at least sit down and explain myself?" I just walked and sat on the couch. Chris sat down across from me on the loveseat.

"I'm listening." This better sound real good, there's only so much that I'm willing to deal with.

"I want to start with telling you that I sincerely apologize to you with all my heart." Chris put her hand over her heart. "You were there for me at my worst, took me and Jordan in, and became the sister that I always wanted. My own sisters have never been there for me. I got caught up in a moment that I know you wouldn't agree with. I wasn't sure how to tell you or what to say. I kept saying to myself, 'I'm going to call,' but every time that I picked up the phone, I froze and put it back down." *I'm feeling like a mother, Chris sounds like a kid in trouble afraid to face her parents. Maybe it's how I come off.*

"Let me tell you how I get down, maybe you don't know me well enough. I'm a friend; I'm not here to judge you on any decisions that you make for your life. I don't have to like them cause guess what, I don't have to live your life. I will always be honest and tell you how I feel about the situation, then I let it go. You never have to play games with me or beat around the bush. I'm going to be straight up with you and you should be able to be straight up with me. Anytime you feel like you have to hide something or anyone, it's not right! Poncho is not my favorite person and in my eyes, not worthy of being with any woman. I don't want that man, been done with him! So, for you to feel like you had to cut me off to be with him is insane!" Chris's eyes damn near popped out of her head. *Yes, I know about you and Poncho. No need in going around it, let's get to it.*

"I see you already know and I should have been the one to tell you." *Let me cut her off before she goes any further.*

"Wait a minute, hold up! You didn't have to tell me because you don't owe me shit! If it ain't Tyson then I don't care who you choose to lay down with. I'm more focused on the friendship, cause can't no dick dictate who I roll with. Don't think that Tyson hasn't tried that, 'I don't want you hanging with Chris, she's bad news,' story, because he has. I had to read him his rights!" Me and Tyson had a big blowout behind her, but it didn't stop me from being her friend. A lot of that had to with that one night stand.

"No, Poncho hasn't said anything about the two of us being friends. He's cool with it. I just felt like I needed to tell you because of how our friendship started. In my weakest moment you came and saved my life. The same man that hurt me so deeply is now making me so happy. He's really changed for the better. He's working on his divorce, spending time with me and Jordan. Poncho has stepped up to the plate in ways I never thought possible. He drops Jordan off at daycare, picks him up, and most nights he puts him to bed. He's being that family man that realized what he lost, and wants it all back. I gave in and gave him a chance, and I'm smiling, Liz. I look at him in amazement sometimes. I feel like I'm in a dream." *Oh no she didn't fall for Poncho and his bullshit. Would I be wrong for busting her bubble? Nope, just like I told her, I have to speak my mind.*

"Chris, Poncho has not changed. Now I'm not an expert on relationships, but I have damn near perfected Poncho and his bullshit! You're talking to someone that knows. I can't count the times I told my family, 'Poncho has changed and it's for real this time.' You have to think with your mind and not your heart. Love will make you see things that aren't really there. When a man comes back right, he's all the way right! Meaning no wife, a job, he takes care of all his kids, not just one! He's doing what he supposed to be doing as a father to his son, it's not like he's breaking a record." I reached over and grabbed Chris's hand. *I feel really for sorry for her. Poncho has done it again, got her brainwashed.*

"I know that. I'm taking a chance and I'm willing to do it. He wants to marry me; we're looking at rings and I'm looking at dresses. This wedding is really happening and he's the one pushing the issue. That's why I'm here…I want you to be my maid of honor!" *What did I just say to her? And she wants to marry him? Ugh, I'm sick to my stomach.*

"Why marry a man that can't take care of you? Well, let me take that back…that doesn't have a job and can't help you. You're taking a hell of a chance. I took one with Tyson because he had the qualities that I wanted in a man. What is Poncho bringing to the table that would even make you remotely want to marry him?" Chris removed her hand from mine.

"Poncho is not all bad. If you just think back I know you can see the good in him. He's helping me take care of Jordan and with the bills. We go out to eat once a week, he had work done on my car and he puts money in my pocket just because." *Now I really think I'm going to throw up.*

"Chris, it's not his money! It's his wife's! And that's okay with you? The man didn't go out here and work or hustle for it! He's still using a woman to get over, and you're sitting here putting him on a pedestal! This is what makes you happy? You're acting as if another woman's downfall is your come up! Poncho is a piece of trash, cruising the streets, that should have been put in the gutter a long time ago!" I'm shaking and loud as shit. I usually try to tone it down because I never want my girls to hear me talk bad about their father.

"I don't care about her. She's getting what she deserves. I don't owe that bitch shit! Why should give I a rat's ass what he does with her money? If he wants to give it to me and spend it on me, then that's her problem, not mine! The bottom line is, I love him and I trust him! I'm marrying Poncho on whatever Saturday following his divorce! I see the change, he's not the man that you knew!" *I don't hear any noise going on upstairs so my nosey kids are probably at the top of the stairs listening to every word.*

"First off, we need to calm this down. All this yelling around my girls ain't good. You sound just like me when I came to a point in the relationship where I was willing to accept whatever chicks came my way. As long as I was number one, I could turn my radar off. There was a time when I needed money for bills and he was coming through for me left and right. That's that hush money, to keep you happy for a minute. When his woman got tired, the money came to a stop and we were broke as can be. You knew about me and continued to mess with him. How do you know that Lisa wasn't put in the same position as you?" I was just speaking some truth to make Chris use her brain.

"This is different. You haven't been with Poncho in years so you really can't say whether he's changed or not. I didn't come over here for a speech on how bad of a person he is. I only wanted to know if you would do me the honor of being my maid of honor in the wedding. Hit me up if you change your mind. I have your dress already picked out, and I want the girls to be in the wedding." Chris got up and walked out the door, leaving me speechless.

*****

I realized I want more for Chris than she wants for herself. After everything that I said she still was gung ho on marrying this man. Now I'm stuck making a decision, do I go ahead and be in this wedding, or do I say hell no? If I say no then I look like the hater that was never a friend to begin with. I'll be accused of still loving and wanting Poncho. That's why I couldn't do it. To hell with what New Haven has to say about me, I just don't want to see her do this, and it has everything to do with her sake, not mine. Either way, people will talk. The ones that know already think that my friendship with Chris is fake and it's not. I have to look at it from a friendship point a view. A friend is there through thick and thin. I'm supposed to support her, and when she falls straight on her face, I'm there to pick her up! No matter how many times she falls, even though I'm totally against it, I'm going to stand up at that altar and smile because of her happiness. When I tell my friends that I ride for them, I really ride for them. *I guess I have a bridal shower and baby shower to plan.*

CHAPTER 15

CHRIS

My life is my life and I'm going to do whatever makes me happy, no matter who's against me. If for some reason Poncho hurts me, it's my price to pay. I'm trusting my man and I believe in him, even if nobody else does. I'm the one in this, the one he talks to each and every day and night. We talk like we've never talked before. Poncho is my best friend. We both want this to work. Our plans are to spend the rest of our lives together. I feel more secure each day, even with Lisa in the picture. When he gets home at night he's on the phone with me. I talk to him on my breaks at work; he even surprises me and drops by my job for lunch. What we have is a love unknown to others, everyone will see in due time.

*****

I fell off for a minute and came home really upset after talking to Liz. Poncho explained to me that what he had with her was puppy love. They were young when they first started out, that he never loved anyone the way he loves me. Once he reassured me, I dried up my tears and got my mind back on what was important to me. It didn't hurt that he made sweet love to me, stroked me up and down something lovely. I almost forgot all about what I was crying for in the first place. *I have to stop letting people get all in my head and just cut them off from the start. If they're not going to have anything nice to say about my relationship, don't say nothing at all.*

I understand where Liz is coming from. It's going to be hard for her to realize that what she had with Poncho was different than what I have with him. He was at a different place in his life. I always saw the potential in him, even when we were creeping. That's what kept me hanging on in the first place. I'm glad I didn't give up on him. He grew up and changed for the better.

*****

As I'm looking out the window I feel chills going through my body watching Poncho and Jordan out front playing in the snow together. We're snowed in, no work or school today. He's such a great father to Jordan now. It wasn't always this way, but now he interacts with him, takes him places, and spends more time with him than me. Jordan is becoming a daddy's little boy for real. Before it was always, 'mommy, mommy, mommy,' now our roles have changed. *What mother wouldn't want this for her son?*

*****

I started dinner early; making some barbecue chicken, mashed potatoes, green beans and cornbread. *Nothing else to do, so I might as well.* I put on my, Mary J, My Life CD, singing along, 'If you look at my life you'll see what I see.' Yeah, that was my jam, and so relevant to exactly what I'm going through. *Maybe once they come in we can watch some kid friendly movies and then when Jordan takes his nap me and Poncho can play some games or something. I wonder if Poncho is going to try to make it home with Lisa or just stay here. I hope he stays here. This is laying up type of weather, and it's supposed to snow until tomorrow. While I'm waiting on this chicken to get done I might as well browse through and look at some more wedding dresses. David's Bridal is having their $99 deal. If I can find a dress for that kind of price then I'm cooking with gas. I found some bridesmaids dresses, but I'm still in limbo about that. My sisters have declined. They both said they wouldn't even be entertaining a mess of a wedding. They're just jealous that nobody would even attempt to marry them.*

Mika should have the baby by the time Poncho gets his divorce. I still haven't heard from her. Liz is going to be my maid of honor, but as of now that's it, besides Keisha. She's working now, so it shouldn't be a problem with her paying for her dress. I could ask Poncho's sisters. He has three of them, but we're not even close. I can count on one hand how many times I've seen them. Jordan doesn't even know them. I am cool with a couple of chicks that I work with; I might just have to ask them. Okay, I'm starting to get stressed already. Planning a wedding ain't no joke.

*****

"Hey you, what you over here thinking about? Got the house smelling all good. Jordan, go take those clothes off in your room. I'll be in there in a minute." Poncho yelled. Jordan was running around like he was still outside, tracking snow all over the floor.

"I'm trying to put this wedding together. I only have Liz and Keisha that are definites." I said with frustration.

"How many more you need?" Poncho asked, sounding concerned for me.

"I need at least three more to match the guys. Let's see, you have Rich and his brother Rob, Quan, Mickey, and Trey. Yep, I need three more ladies." Poncho bent down and kissed me on the lips.

"Don't worry about it. I'll get them. Mickey, Quan, and Trey all have girlfriends; we can make it a couple's thang. There's your three right there. That's a small thing. Don't be getting all stressed out over nothing. I'm going to see what Jordan is in there doing and get out of these wet clothes. Be right back." *This is why I love this man. He's so loving, caring and understanding. Just like that, problem solved. This is what I'm talking about, the things that he does for me that people don't see. I feel so much better now. He's far from perfect, and yes he's made a lot of mistakes, but who hasn't? Life is a journey that we live and learn from. Let me shut down my laptop. I don't want Poncho to see the dresses that I'm looking at. I'm going to make a beautiful bride.*

*****

"You okay now, Sweetie? I hope I took some of the load off you." Poncho picked me up from the kitchen chair carrying me into the living room.

"Yes, I'm much better." I looked him eye to eye. "You make me so happy and I love you so much!" He gently put me down on the couch and sat right next to me.

Grabbing my face he said, "I'm glad, and I told you I'm not out to hurt you! I love you more than life itself. We're going to be okay, fuck everybody else! We're in this thing together, no matter what. Who cares if your mother or sisters don't come? I don't want them there anyway, if they're not going to be happy for us!" Yeah, he's been telling me this, but I keep trying to push the issue. I want my immediate family there. I always pictured my mother giving me away, but now I have to settle for my uncle. I'm hurt, but it's her loss. *Maybe if my mother wasn't such a ho, I would know who my father is and he could give me away.*

"You're right, I just want everything to be perfect. I have my aunts doing the cooking, and you know they can throw down in the kitchen. I'm thinking fried and baked chicken, meatballs, potato and macaroni salad, tossed salad, green beans, corn, baked macaroni & cheese, rice, and rolls. What do you think?" I got up and walked into to the kitchen to check on my barbecue chicken. *Mmmm, yummy!* It was nice and done, falling off the bones. I pulled it out, set it on top of the stove, turned the oven off and made my way back into the living room to get Poncho's input on the menu.

"I think that's too much food. Why do we have to give them a full course meal? Can't we keep it simple, like some wingettes or something?" *Oh no sweetie! What kind of wedding did he have with Lisa? This wedding will be done up in class.*

"No, we need to give them a full course meal, not some ghetto ass food! I want everyone to be nice and full while they're having a good time. It's our special day, so why should we settle?" Poncho was giving me that puppy eyed look and I was pouting to get my way.

"Whatever you want," Poncho threw his hands up in the air. "I think we need to set a date! I talked to my lawyer and the divorce should be final within the next couple of months!" I screamed out loud. *Finally, it's moving along.*

"You have no idea what you just did to me right now! Poncho, I am so excited. We can actually set a date. I want to do it early Spring, like March or April." *I prefer the warmer weather.*

"That a long time, it's only November! I was figuring after the holidays, like sometime in January." *Is he crazy? I can't put a wedding together in such a short time, plus do Thanksgiving, Christmas and New Years.*

"Ugh, Bae, that's unrealistic…weddings take time. I'm not going to do what Lisa did and just throw something together. I want it to be right." *Spring will be here before we even know it. I wanted to do it as soon as his divorce was final, but I thought it would take longer that this.*

"Okay, do it your way! I want it to be right too. Enough of this wedding talk. Seeing that we're snowed in together, what are we going to do, besides eat?" Poncho winked his eyes at me. *I know what's on his mind.*

"I thought we could watch a couple of movies with Jordan. Where is he anyway? He's too quiet!" I started to peep in his room when Poncho grabbed me.

"I wore his little ass out. He's sleeping. You do know what that means, don't you?" Aww man, I thought we were going to save this for later on tonight. I don't know what's getting into Poncho; my legs stay in the air. He desires me more and more each day.

"Okay, but I can't be loud, you know what Jordan told my mom. Come on, Daddy!" I grabbed Poncho by the hand and led him into our bedroom.

CHAPTER 16

THE BUM SQUAD

PONCHO

I'm in over my head with these women. Planning two weddings and a divorce party. I just need a break from it all. Honesty and Chris are coming at me hard with this wedding stuff. Wifey is threatening to cut my credit cards off, and I'm threatening to tell her people that's she don't like no dick. Home is really crazy right now. All we do is argue. I try my best to stay out of Lisa's way, half the time I'm not there anyway. She had a fit when I left her by herself for the two days that I was snowed in with Chris. Why, I don't know!

*****

Honesty was pissed off that she didn't hear from me. I turned my phone off, told her that I couldn't find my charger. Lisa already knew that I was laid up somewhere doing me.

*****

My schedule is kind of busy. I drop Jordan off in the morning then I spend most of my day with Honesty. Chris gets her first fifteen-minute break at ten, and like clockwork she calls. Well, that's my time to hit the bathroom claiming to take my daily shit. I sit in there and talk to her unless Honesty is trying to play eye-spy. Normally, I'm just finishing up from rocking her world, so she's still lying in bed with her legs shaking. Then at noon, Chris goes on lunch. By then I'm out picking up food for me and Honesty, unless she has something to do, then I go meet up with Chris and have lunch with her. Chris gets her last fifteen-minute break at two. By then I'm gone from Honesty's, and I'm meeting up with the squad until it's time to pick up Jordan from the daycare. I usually leave them around four, pick up Jordan by four-thirty and bring him home. Then I stay with Chris and Jordan until around nine or ten, then head home. That's my Monday through Friday schedule.

My weekends are planned accordingly. I could be anywhere. From chilling with Honesty in Bridgeport, to running errands with Chris, it just depends. I still do my Sunday ritual, meet wifey at church and fake the funk.

I haven't been home to eat Sunday dinner since I caught wifey with Honesty. Chris cooks Sunday dinner, so usually I hang out with her until after I eat, then I leave, bring Honesty her plate, chill for a few, and get home when I get there. Honesty doesn't cook. She always wants to eat out. She's killing my pockets and credit cards. Her rent needs to be paid, along with bills. I can't pay any of them with the credit cards because when wifey gets the bill she will automatically know, since she used to pay them.

I've been managing to scam money out of wifey, but that's all about to come to an end because I'm tired of taking care of Honesty. I'm used to being a kept man. One thing I don't do is take care of a woman, wrong dude. Honesty better get a job. I told her there's no reason why she can't work. *She's busy planning this wedding when she needs to be planning for a job.*

*****

I'm going against the grain on marrying these two women. I said I was going for bigger and better, with more money. Now I'm going to have to find me a side piece with the dough. This time I will scout out a more mature woman with wisdom. Less maintenance for me, and we both get what we want. All she's going to want is for me to beat it up and go about my business. It sure will be my pleasure and I won't have to worry about her getting her period. It doesn't matter to me, but Chris and Honesty make a big deal out it, it's like pulling teeth to get some. Just take a bath and lay a towel down. Plus, they both get it around the same time, putting me out of commission for a week. That's definitely a problem for me. I like to go and go; I never get tired of serving the sweet spot.

That's the reason why God put me here in the first place. It's my calling and purpose in life. A man was never meant to be with just one woman anyway.

Women kill me how they expect all this faithfulness with all this ass, hips, and titties out here shaking in these streets. It's too tempting for any man to deal with. Eventually, he will fall weak and that third leg starts doing the thinking. Women need to wake up and realize that if you want a relationship with a man, then expect to be cheated on at one time or another. Just close them eyes and act like you don't see anything. God should have made women blind, then us men wouldn't have to worry about ducking and dodging all the damn time. That would have been the smart thing to do. *Lord, what were you thinking?*

*****

I'm sitting outside Honesty's apartment, trying to gather my thoughts before I go in, not knowing what I'm in for today, and it's not our usual time that we meet up. I told Chris I had something to take care of, texted Honesty and told her I was dropping by; that we needed to talk. With all this running around back and forth between the two, I had to come up with a plan that would help me out a little. *Honesty needs to take her broke ass back to the Port. That will save me time and money.* A brother needs to know just what kind of wife she's trying to be. We can just kick it if she wants to, but I'm not buying no ring for her to be sitting around on her ass. Don't get me wrong, she's kinky in the bedroom and one of the best freaks I've

123

ever had, but she needs other womanly skills. Like getting down in that kitchen preparing a meal and shit.

I happen to look up and see Honesty walking this dude out of her apartment. The apartment where I'm paying the rent and bills. *I know she ain't that stupid to have somebody up in there. I'm going to sit here and watch this play out. I don't want to jump the gun. It could be nothing, but if it is something, I'm going to find out. She must have noticed me sitting out here.* Next thing I know she's walking up to my car. *Okay, it must not be nothing.* Dude is walking in the other direction not paying me no mind. I unlock the door so she can get it in.

*****

"Hey, what's up?" Honesty asked.

"I don't know, you tell me. Who is old dude that was just in your apartment?" *Damn he looks raggedy. Jeans I never heard of, sagging off his ass, sneakers all dirty, and hoodie on with no coat. Man, it's too cold for that. He must not have far to go.*

"Oh, that's my cousin, Champ! He just moved down here not too long ago. Remember I told you about him. The one that said he doesn't like you." *Oh yeah, I do remember that conversation. Fuck him!*

"You should have introduced me to him. Once he gets to know me he'll change his mind." *Even if he don't, I'm not sweating him. He's mad because Honesty confided in him when she found out that I was married to Lisa. Like he ain't a man. He should know how we do!*

"Um yeah, I didn't want no problems. So what was it that you wanted to talk to me about?" Honesty turned around, looking at me smiling. *Let's see if that smile disappears or not.*

"Well, since we're planning this wedding and you're about to be my wife, we need to discuss our future together. The first thing I need to know is how you're going to pay your rent this month?" *Yep, I knew it. The smile disappeared and turned into a frown.*

"Well, I guess I need a job. I've never really worked anywhere. I don't even know where to start." *Now I find out that she's been lying to me? She told me that she's been putting in applications all over, but nobody has called her back. Of course you're not gonna get a call back if you haven't even started looking. She's taking me for a joke. Both of us can't not work, and I'm not working under any circumstances. I can always find me a place to lay my head. I can see now that I will be moving in with Chris and Honesty will be my part time wife.*

"You only have two weeks to come up with the rent, and I'm all tapped out. Lisa is not giving me any more money. She cut off all my credit cards, leaving me flat broke." *Yep, I'm on my best bullshit. Picture that happening. I got Lisa by the balls that she wish she had.*

"Shit! You can't talk to her and make something happen? What am I going to do? I have to come up with that money!" *Yeah, that's what I want to know. What are you going to do? Oh I know you're going to take your ass right back where you came from until you can do better.*

"I don't know. You might have to go back to the Port for a little while, where your family is, until we can afford to get our own place." *Honesty better recognize a thing or two. If I'm going to marry a woman with no job experience then she gets what I give. Since she wants to be a minimum wage wife, she get's treated as such. I'm not a minimum wage husband. She has to step her game up ten notches.*

"Well how long is it gonna take you to get us a place? And when are you getting a job? The husband is supposed to take care of the wife. All I do is help you." *I'll be damned! Tables have turned. What world is she living in? I'm going to be the one helping when I can.*

"That all depends on how long it takes you to get a job and save up some money. I been footing the bill, now I need you to return the favor. I'm here to help you. You know I can't get no job with child support coming after me. One of us needs some steady income. I'm going to start doing side jobs, but it won't be nothing steady." *My side jobs will be my other women, but she won't know it.*

"Are you still going to pay for the wedding?" Honesty asked, looking all pitiful.

"Yeah, yeah, yeah, your family said they're going to help too. It might not be as extravagant as we want it to be, but it will be a little something. Are you sure you want to be my wife?" *Of course she does, just like every woman out here. It's my way of getting down to what I'm really trying to say before we jump over this broom. Honesty has to be molded into a wife.*

"Yes, why would you even ask me a question like that? I found my dress and my cousins put the down payment on their bridesmaid dresses. I'm so excited, like I can't believe I'm going to a wife." *Well, that makes two of us. I can't believe it either.*

"The reason I asked is because I'm expecting some things out of you. I need a hot meal when I come in the house. You have to get them cooking skills in order. I need you to be career driven. No man wants a lazy wife. Maybe you could go to work and school at the same time. Find something that you love to do, besides me." I laughed to take some of the pressure off of her.

"I understand. I'll start looking into it once I get back up to the Port. My uncle is an awesome cook. He does it for a living. I can get him to teach me about some food and he might even get me a job at the restaurant that he works for." *Now we're talking. Some women just need a little push in the right direction, and she's going back! Yes, winning!*

"That will work, sunshine. I want you to be all that you can be. We only get one shot at life, and I'm putting myself out there once again, but this time with somebody that I love. I want our marriage to work, don't you?" *I'll say whatever is going to work to get that ass moving in the right direction.*

"Yes baby. Just promise me that once I move back to Bridgeport that things are still going to be the same; that you won't cheat on me with one of these other chicks. Can I trust you down here without me?" *Oh yeah, that million-dollar question that women can't really handle the answer to. If you have to ask then you should already know. Hell no! I'm not faithful now.*

"Yes, sunshine, these other chicks out here are not worth me losing you. *(Singing)* *'Say my lady/ You are so fine/ I wake up in the mornin' to see a smile on your face (baby)/ You are the queen of my heart baby/ I belong to you and you belong to me (yeah)/ Girl you are the love of my life baby/ All those cloudy days they fade away when you come my way baby.'* Those words speak from my heart. I know I can't sing, but see what you do to me. Got me over here singing. My boys would kill me if they found out." *This is how you do it. I got Honesty over here crying.*

"I've never had a man sing to me before. Now I know how you really feel about me. I like the softer side of you. I feel so special and I have this warmth inside of my heart for you that I can't explain. Let's go inside, baby. I want to make love." *Okay then! She didn't have to ask me once. I knew what I was doing. She's going to give it to me real good. Making a woman feel special makes her perform way better than on a normal day.*

CHAPTER 17

THE BUM SQUAD

RICH

Since I've been away from Dominique, I've been helping
Keisha try to obtain custody of the kids. Once DCF pulls my
background I won't stand a chance. My charges are still pending,
who knows how long the New Haven court will drag this out. Right
now I have a public defender named Ms. Reynolds that ain't worth
shit. If I didn't know any better I would think that she's the
prosecutor. She tried to get me to take a plea deal of two years with
five years probation on top of that. I wouldn't be able to see my kids
without supervision. To me, that ain't no plea, it's a death trap.
She's bringing up my past record but I haven't been in trouble in a
minute, and this isn't for drugs. This is domestic; as far as I'm
concerned, it's my first offense. When I tried to tell her that I was

provoked, she just brushed me off like I was lying. That's when I knew I needed to get me some proper representation. I told Ms. Reynolds to get me a continuation cause I wasn't copping out to no plea. Now I'm on the hunt for a worthy lawyer that's talking my language. Dominique ain't getting me caught out like that! I may have been wrong, but don't lead me on even to think that I had a chance when she knew damn well she wasn't going to forgive me. Don't use me to help you out for your convenience when I gave it my all this time. Women are always accusing us men of being liars when they're the biggest liars; the lies are just hidden in their hearts.

*****

Keisha should be getting the kids back any day now. She's been in full compliance with DCF, going above and beyond. She was working two jobs, McDonald's and Popeyes. She had to let one go because of DCF and their strict guidelines. Too much time away from the kids makes her unfit. They got Keisha a three-bedroom apartment on Orchard Street that goes by her income. A program like Section 8, except it's called RAP (Rental Assistance Program). Plus they gave her furniture vouchers to have the necessities that she needs. Her food stamps are back in full effect, along with the WIC vouchers. The system set her up with no options to fail.

If I wasn't gung-ho on getting back with Dominique, then I could be in the same position. *Now look at my stupid ass!* Living with Rob and his psychotic wife, driving me crazy, and my badass nieces and nephew. I have to constantly bite my tongue and humble myself. If I get out of line they will throw me out to the wolves. It's too cold in New England for me to be living on the streets. I stay gone as much as I can to avoid any kind of confusion, plus I pay them rent.

Keisha wants me to move in with her, but I can't do that with DCF popping up whenever they feel like it. I might be able to finagle some shit, but I'll take a pass. Things are good just the way they are. Leading Keisha on to even think that we're in a relationship would be a heavy mistake on my part. I'm just going to be one of those baby daddy's that can always come around to make a hit and run.

*****

Keisha is feeling herself, switching all up. Getting paid every week, gaining confidence in herself, trying to act all brand new. Buying herself clothes, going to get her hair and nails done. Acting like she's Queen K. It's okay though. She looks better than she ever did. Now you can see her real beauty. Before I just paid attention to her banging ass body, but now she got me doing double takes. With the right weave, decent clothes, and some boots on her feet; I hate to say this, but she's one of them chicks that can shut New Haven down. I may be going a little overboard because I know how she handles herself in the bedroom. She ain't dirty Keisha no more, she's the new and improved Keisha. When she opens her mouth you still get the same Keisha. She's still ghetto as hell, not lady-like at all. As long as she don't talk and you looking on the outside, the package is pretty nice. Oh yeah, she's getting that much needed attention that she never got. I'm not jealous and the shit doesn't effect me, as long I'm getting served right.

I learned my lesson after the third pregnancy; I'm not running up in Keisha raw. She claims she's getting that Depo shot, but I'm not taking any chances. As much as I want to hit it raw, I think about the responsibility that comes with it, and I say 'Hell no.' Those condoms are good enough for me. Anything is better than using my hand and imagination. I was trying my pull out game, but every time I left her I never felt safe, always paranoid about my baby number four.

✳✳✳✳✳

I have no idea why Dominique is calling me. Something better be wrong with one of my kids, bitch has no business contacting me. "What?"

"Now that's nerve answering the phone like that, I'm the one with missing teeth!" *I see Dominique is still playing victim.*

"What do you want? We're not supposed to have any contact, yo!" *I'm just making myself clear. She might be trying to throw me up under the bus.*

"Well, I'm calling you about our kids, you need to talk to them. They're terrified of you. At this point they want nothing to do with you! All I've been doing is reassuring them that you would never lose your temper and mind with them!" *She should have been thinking about all of this before she got it twisted.*

"I'll straighten that out after this court mess, but from now on, I'm going by the law! Did you explain to the kids why I lost it? Have they met mommy's boyfriend yet?" *I guarantee she didn't tell the kids all of that, but she can bet on my last dollar that I will. Let's see how she likes that!*

"The kids don't need to know everything because they're still too young to understand. All they know is that they saw their father beating the shit out of their mother. No matter what I try to tell them, they know what their eyes seen. You need to apologize to them in person." *Aww hell no! In person? How, when I have a restraining order?*

"Did you forget, that I can't be within three hundred feet of you or the kids? Like I said, that will have to wait until I can establish some visitation. Please go ahead and start the divorce papers, I'm ready to be free legally." *The sooner we wrap this up, the better for me. I keep picturing her and new dude in my head and that's a situation that will have me catching a case. Once we get divorced he can have her openly, but as long she still carrying my last name, fuck no!*

"Oh what happened to, 'I'm never signing shit. Dominique I love you and the kids'? Now your tune has changed. Whatever, man! You've been doing you anyway, being married to me never made a difference." *Yeah well, that all changed when you let another dick enter into you.*

"You right, but you did hear the legally part or did that just fly over your head? This way, when the time is right, I can propose to a woman that's going to appreciate me. Second time around I want to do things right. Oh, and I'll be introducing the kids to their other brothers and sister. Keisha's doing real good; she changed her life around. Have you seen her lately? She looks damn good!" *The right words will always set it off.*

"FUCK YOU! FUCK YOU, YOU SORRY ASS BASTARD!" Next thing I know there was a click. *Aww, poor Dominique hung up on me. That's exactly how I want her, pissed off and hurt!*

CHAPTER 18

LIZ

"Baby, don't take this the wrong way, but you have some dumb ass friends." Tyson was digging in my ass. He likes to wait until it's time to go to bed to start some mess. *All I want to do is get a good night's rest so I can get up and go to work in the morning.*

"Why, because I'm going to be the maid of honor in my baby daddy's wedding?" I don't think it's dumb; Chris and I are cool. What's the big deal?" I rolled my eyes at him.

"It's not just that, they're all a bunch of nutcases. I keep telling you to be more careful of the people that you're connected to. Why can't my woman have normal friends? The kind of friends that don't come with a whole lot of drama." Tyson loves arguing over my friends. It seems like it's the only fault that he finds in me.

"You want me to cut all my friends off, just so you can have me to yourself. That's so selfish. I don't say anything when you go hang out with your boys!" I rolled over, no longer facing him.

"Don't turn your back on me! The truth hurts, that's all! My boys don't bring me no drama. When have I ever came home with a problem stemming from one of them? Never! They know better than to involve me in any of their bullshit. I'm telling you right now, we are not going to make it, because of your friends. Every time they have a problem, you bring it home! The only one that I halfway like is Mika!" *Hmm that's funny, last time I checked, you agreed to be the godfather of the baby of someone that you halfway like. Nice Tyson! Let your true feelings come out now that we have committed to this baby.*

"My friends are my friends, Tyson, and none of them have done a damn thing to you for you not to like them. You're just wrong on so many levels." *He's right, this won't work, ain't no man picking and choosing who I deal with it. That's a control issue and I won't be controlled.*

"I'm wrong for wanting you to hang with women that have some class? Women that have some respect for themselves. You think I want my future wife to be attached to a bunch of women that have low self-esteem and are hard up for a man! Naw, I want you with women that are sure of themselves, women that don't mind being alone because they know that a man can't make them. Positive females doing positive things. You need to hang with women that will help uplift you and not have you crying with them all the damn time! That's the shit I'm talking about!" *One thing I can't stand is a judgmental man.*

"Listen, you are so quick to criticize my friends but have you forgotten that you fucked one? She can't be too bad of a person. You don't know all of their stories, just bits and pieces! There's a reason for everything, and I look at the deeper issue and not just what's thrown in front me." *He just needs to mind his own business and not worry about what's going on with my friends. I stopped volunteering information, now he asks all the questions. If he wasn't being so nosey then he wouldn't know shit, but I bet you one thing...even when he asks, from now my answers will always be everything is fine.*

"I'm not with her either. You said it right; I fucked her, because that's all she was, a fuck! I chose to deal with your broken ass because I saw something in you. If you wanted to be a counselor and fix people, then you should go practice in the field of expertise. Open up a non-profit for broken hearted females that can't seem to catch a good man if you paid them to!" Tyson wanted my full attention and he surely got it. I turned myself around looking him dead in the face. *Did this fool just call me a broken ass?*

"Who's the broken ass?" Tyson looked stuck, as if it that just slipped out of his mouth. "I asked you a question, who's the broken ass?

"Well when I met you, you were broken. Afraid of this, afraid of that, insecure, terrified of opening your heart up, like every man was out to get you! All you women have to do is pay attention to the quality of men that you are attracted to. When you met me you didn't have to put me together, I was already made. When you want that smooth talker, no job having ass man, that's what you get. A man that will continue to talk and not be about shit." *He really needs to watch how he talks to me. I was a put together woman that wasn't willing to be heartbroken by any man, period. Just because Tyson had a job and place did not make me jump and assume that he was a good man. First of all, if he didn't have any of that, conversation was over from the start.*

"Excuse me, I wasn't broken. I wasn't just going to lay down or jump into any relationship just to say I had a man. You're lucky that I gave you a chance!" I sat up on the bed now. *This conversation was getting heated. I could see now that I would be sleeping on the couch and looking for a place for me and my girls tomorrow. I'll bounce on his ass like it ain't nothing. He's not gonna sit here and act like he did me a favor by being in my life. I'm an asset that's very sure of myself!*

"You know what they say, if you hang with a Ho then you must be a Ho. I'm just using that as an example. You are whoever you hang with! All your friends have one thing in common, bum ass niggas, cause that's what they like! Then when he breaks their little hearts they come running to you for advice that you already gave them in the first place. Some people you need to outgrow and love them from a distance. They're not on your level, but you choose to still be there. There's a reason why these celebrities leave people behind. You have to change your mentality. Now let's say we get married, are we going to still be dealing with all these single people, or are we going to be dealing with other married couples that can help us along the way? What advice can any of your friends give us? Not one of them is with a decent man!" *There was a time when I was single and by myself, now he wants me to act like that part of my life didn't exist. If things go sour with me and him, then who's shoulder can I cry on after I kick my friends to the curb? He's crazy. I'm not turning my back on my friends.*

"You're making my friends out to be the worst women in the world, and they're not. They want to be happy!" Tyson interrupted me before I could finish the point I was trying to make.

"Let me cut you off right there. When a person wants to be happy they go find happiness and that doesn't always include a man. Your friends list goes like this: first there is Mika, who's pregnant by your baby daddy's best friend. Dude don't even know that he has a baby on the way. Wrong! Now baby boy is messed up because daddy never been there, but daddy never even knew about baby boy. Baby boy also has brothers and sisters floating around New Haven that one day he will walk by, not even knowing that they share the same DNA. All because she's mad that she was messing with a married man in the first place, that lied to her. Then she finds out about his other baby mama, which happens to be his wife's cousin, but he's the dog who did her wrong! Then there's that news reporter, Wanda. All up in everybody's business until she got some of her own. Waited on a dude, for over ten years, to come home from jail, assuming she had a future with a man that was locked up in the first place. She puts her life on hold like she's going to live forever and has time to waste. All she had to do was say, 'Look man, you got too much time on your hands. I love you but I can't do this bid with you. If you come home and I'm still single then we can hook up!' Any real man would never ask a woman to wait for him, knowing he has that much time. Now she's getting back to the norm, minding everyone else's business again. Meddling in people's lives, starting shit all over New Haven. Now there's Chris. Both of y'all have the same baby daddy and became cool over baby daddy breaking her heart by marrying his come up while he was with her. Then she has the nerve to go back to being side chick, engaged to a married man, wants you to be the maid of honor in this bogus ass wedding, that you really don't want to be in in the first place. But you'll do it because of your loyalty. But when you were calling and texting her, where was her loyalty? You got kicked to the curb until she got up enough nerve to come clean, and I'm supposed to sit here and attend this wedding to support my woman. I don't have dinner because you been running around all week trying to plan a baby shower and a bridal shower. Your family is being neglected behind your ratchet ass friends. We already had this conversation, I'm not about to argue with you over the same shit. If I wife you up, these are the things that I would have to deal with because of the company that you choose to keep. You have to ask yourself, are they worth it? Then you can let me know where I stand!" *I can't stand when I confide in a person and they throw it back up in my face. So what, my friends have made some mistakes. I'm supposed to cut them off for him. Why should I? Five days of me not cooking caused all of this? This is some bullshit! He doesn't need me to cook. Tyson can cook.*

"You gave me this long ass speech because you and the kids didn't have dinner made this week? So you can never be inconvenienced? Tyson, that's just plain old selfish, selfish, selfish! I get tired of coming home, cooking every night, cleaning up and washing clothes. Am I not entitled to a break sometimes? I don't say nothing when you go riding with the fellas or go meet up for a beer. You never hear my mouth!" I got up grabbed my blanket and snatched my pillow off the bed. *Downstairs on the couch was looking better and better.*

"Oh, you are entitled to a break. Everyone is, and you get them. Sometimes you come home and dinner is cooked, house cleaned, clothes washed, homework done, and baths taken. I give you all of that! The only reason why you do the majority is because you get home before me now, because I've been working a lot of overtime. When you don't feel like cooking, we order out. But a whole week is ridiculous. You're not sick! You're too busy running around making sure that your friends' shit is right. Make sure home is straight first! When I hang out with my friends I always let you know in advance and ask if you have anything planned? Is it okay? Do you need me for anything? I don't get that from you, and I'm not playing second to some bitches that don't do shit for you!"

CHAPTER 19

CHRIS

Poncho is watching Jordan while I get some Thanksgiving shopping done. My first stop is Ferraro's. *I hate this store. It's always so crowded, but they have the best deals on meat.* I'm trying to find somewhere to park. *Luckily this car is pulling out so I can pull in.* I made my list before I left the house. I need to make sure I get everything while I'm out.

Poncho wants me to make a small turkey, ham, chopped barbecue, prime rib, baked mac and cheese, homemade mashed potatoes, yams, collard greens, corn on the cob, sweet potato pies, and bake a cake…and it's only the three of us. *Who's going to eat all this food?*

I invited Liz, Tyson, and the kids to come over. Might as well, since my mother and sisters turned me down once again. Nobody wants to be around Poncho, I guess, but they need to get used to it because he's not going anywhere. I would invite Mika but she's been too salty towards me, so I scratched that name off the list and invited Rich, Keisha, and their kids, since Keisha has them back now. This way Keisha won't have to worry about cooking Thanksgiving dinner, just enjoy her children.

Liz did confirm that she was coming, but that Tyson was having dinner with his family. I smell some trouble brewing. I would think, that since this is their first holiday together in the house, they would at least be spending it together. It could just be me overthinking, or maybe I'm just a hopeless romantic.

I agreed to let Poncho have the day to himself and make his rounds, but dinner is at four. *He better there on time and hungry.* This is his personal request list and I'm not trying to hear that he ate somewhere else. *Now that I have all the meats, it's time to stand in this long line. Why is this chick staring me up down like she's knows me or something?*

*****

"Hello, do I know you?" I'm not the type to just let you stare at me without speaking.

"Probably not, but I know you!" *She looks a little familiar but I can't put my finger on it.* My mind is in overdrive.

"Where you know me from?" I asked, still trying to be polite, ignoring the way she was looking at me. *She looked like she had some kind of beef with me. If I didn't have a carriage full I might ask her to take this outside.*

"I'm Lisa, Poncho's wife!" *Damn, I should have known. I couldn't put one and two together fast enough.*

"Oh, how are you doing?" I smiled like, 'Bitch if you don't get your homey ass away from me...'"

"Now that I see you, I'm much better. Thank you for taking my husband off my hands, most of the time anyway. But he still has that itch for me, if you know what I mean. How is he anyway? Since I haven't seen in the past week, I'm assuming he's been at your house!" My whole facial expression changed straight to an angry bitch. *Poncho has been leaving me every night, but where the fuck was he was sleeping if it wasn't home? She can say what she wants, I know for a fact that he ain't fucking her. Not with the way he be digging in my ass every day.*

"He's fine. Right now he's with our son while I'm getting our dinner together for Thanksgiving. I'll let him know that you asked for him. It was nice meeting you." The line was moving, but this bitch wouldn't get out of my way. *I'm in a hurry to get home and find out where Poncho has been all week. I can't even think straight right now. He's back to playing his little games.*

"I'm not done with you yet, Miss Chris! There are a couple more things that I need to discuss with you, and make sure that we are clear on. He's over there with you by my choice. I gave you your dog back. He wasn't what or who I thought he was. I've been doing a little checking on my husbands whereabouts, so that when I go to court I will have a substantial amount of evidence to walk away from this marriage without losing a dime. On that note, you just lied to me and told me that he's been with you. He hasn't been with you; I just wanted to see what you would say. He's been in Bridgeport with his other bitch that you don't know about. Tell him I said come see me before the devil comes out in me!" *Oh no, this bitch just walked off leaving her cart of food. Guess what? So am I. We're both going out this door.*

"Excuse me, excuse me!" The old maid finally turned around and looked my way. "Poncho was with me before you were ever thought about. Before you jumped up and married a man that was already taken, that's when you should have sent your goons out to investigate!"

"Oh sweetie, you think I didn't know about you? Trust me, I did my homework. But it was pretty clear to me that you were nothing more than a baby mama. I guess I could call you that fallback chick with reliable pussy! Lord, forgive me for talking in such filthy language. See, I never slept with Poncho until our wedding night. He fell for me without me even giving up my jewels." She left me no other choice but to laugh in her face and check that ass. *Running around thinking because she saved herself before marriage that makes her better than me. Poncho ain't waiting on no ass. He was in my bed not missing a beat.*

"No, you homey bitch, he fell for your pocketbook. You know those credit cards that we use and the cash that we spend. You might be married to him for now. I'm not in the business of buying a husband, because that's exactly what you did. I do however, enjoy spending your money." I didn't realize how loud I was until I heard the crowd saying, 'Damn'. I looked around at a busy parking lot that came to a standstill. This is New Haven for you, something going on and everybody stops to gather around instead of going about their business. All I can do is shake my head at this point.

"The God that I serve will have his way with you. I hope you enjoy the debt that you're incurring because you will be paying back every single dollar that you've ever spent. Any debt that I have is his debt. Now that I'm adding to our family and having my husband's baby, I will be keeping my house and I might require a little bit of child support." Lisa had the nerve to rub her stomach, jump in her car, and pull off.

*****

I'm pissed off to the tenth power. Veins popping out my head, red like a lobster, and my whole body shaking like I have tourette syndrome. I can barely control the wheel of my car. I'm so hot right now that I could start a fire without a match. *Poncho has played me once again and has me looking like a fool. When will I learn that this man will never change? My mother was right, Liz was right, so were my sisters. Hell, everyone was right, except me. He's been gone all week with some cunt in Bridgeport while I was thinking that he was home with the Old Maid. Now he has another baby on the way? I'm going to kill him this time! If he wasn't fucking his wife, then how in the hell did she get pregnant? He lied to me! It was all a bunch of lies!*

I was so sick to my stomach that I started throwing up on the ride home. *I have to pull over, not that I want to stop this car, but if I don't I'll probably kill myself before I can even get to him. This pain is worse than when I found out that he got married on me. Sure didn't think that could happen. I can't even shed a tear; the tears won't leave my eyes.* Now that I halfway finished throwing up my guts, back on the road I go, rushing to get home. A fifteen-minute ride felt like fifteen hours.

I pull up to the house and make sure I see his beamer sitting outside, looking all pretty. *It won't look like that by the time I'm done. That shit is going to the motherfucking junkyard!* I jump out the car and run up the stairs all out of breath. My hands are shaking so bad that I can't even get the key to unlock the door. Poncho swings the door open.

*****

"Honey, what's wrong with you? Are you okay, you sick?" I glanced down at myself. Not only did I have vomit all over me, I accidently peed on myself too. *Oh my God, my nerves are shot!*

I immediately charged at him, head first right into his stomach, pushing the kitchen table up against the window, chairs go flying and Jordan is screaming, 'Mommy, Mommy, Mommy!' *Not now Jordan, you're just gonna have to watch me kill your father.*

"Chris, what the fuck is wrong with you?" Poncho grabbed me, having total control.

"Yeah mommy, what the fluck is wrong with you?" Jordan repeated.

"Poncho, let go of me!" I'm lying on the kitchen floor with Poncho on top of me, holding me down from killing his ass!

"I met your pregnant wife today, the one you claim you ain't fucking! Your ass been in Bridgeport creeping every night this week when you had me thinking that you were going home! Once again, you broke my heart, Poncho!" Now I could feel the tears coming down hitting my cheeks.

"Chris, I told you I was getting real tired of this shit! You go out here and believe a bitch that doesn't even see her husband because most of the time I'm with you! I call you before I go in the house and I text you 'good night' every night when I'm going to sleep! Where is my dick? My dick is married to you because every time you look around it's up in you! Lisa is the one mad and angry, and you let her get to you! If she's pregnant it ain't by me. I swear I haven't touched her! The bitch don't see me because I go in the basement, where my man cave is!" Poncho rolled over and slowly got up off the floor looking at me with tears in his eyes.

"Well she s…"

"I don't give a flying fuck what she said, he said, or what the fuck the world said! I know what I said. The plans that we made together. But this right here," Poncho shook his head. "You can't trust me. Our past will always cause us problems. I'm walking out this door; all bets are off! I gave it my very best shot, Chris, I'm not doing this anymore." Poncho picked up Jordan to stop him from crying. "I love you son. Daddy will always be here for you, but mommy needs her space right now. I'm going to come to the daycare to see you every day, okay?" Jordan shook his head.

"Mommy, you made daddy mad!" Jordan screamed.

"Poncho, don't leave me. I'm so sorry! I did let her get to me, what was I supposed to do? How would you feel if my husband walked up on you?" I was trying to help Poncho see things from my eyes.

"If the roles were reversed Chris, I would have chose you and not the lies that were being told!" Poncho put Jordan down, kissed him on the cheek, gave him a high five and walked out the door.

"PONCHO, DON'T LEAVE! PONCHO, I LOVE YOU! PONCHO!" I opened up the door, running down the steps, screaming from the top of my lungs.

CHAPTER 20

THE BUM SQUAD

RICH

*W*omen are the route to all evil and the weakness to my balls. You know how the saying goes, 'Can't live with them, can't live without them.' The whole world revolves around a damn woman.

*****

Dominique is a piece of work. As soon as I hung up the phone on her, she went to find Keisha. Starting shit at her job. Good thing it was only McDonald's and Keisha was cool with the manger, or else she would have been fired. Dominique went up there carrying on about my kids and how Keisha lied to her. *So what?* They get into a fight again, started from the inside, then ended up on the outside. From what I heard they were going blow for blow.

Keisha's weave was tore up, face all scratched up, and Dominique lost another tooth. By the time I got there everything was over. And the law wasn't called, which was a good thing. But I did have to hear Keisha's mouth running off a mile a minute about, 'Why did I tell Dominique without discussing it with her first?' So I said to Keisha, 'The same reason why you didn't tell me about you wanting to get pregnant three times.' *Why did I say that?* Next thing I know Keisha's five knuckles was in my damn mouth. I'm out there in the parking lot trying to stop this girl from swinging on me, slipped on some ice, sprained my foot and dislocated my shoulder. I'm out of work, on crutches and in a sling for the next six to eight weeks. I called my lawyer though, McDonald's will be paying me. *I slipped and fell on their property, that's all they need to know.* My lawyer has me in therapy three times a week. *Cha ching! I can't wait to cash that check.*

*****

Unfortunately, I've been forced to stay with Keisha since I can barely wash my ass without help. *As soon as I get a little better and can drive, I'm out of here.* She's been over here thinking that we're on some family shit. *Aww hell naw, we ain't. This is just a temporary situation.* I can see it's getting to her big ass head. She's catering to me like I'm her man, feeding me, bathing me, helping me get dressed, making sure I take my meds and checking on me every five minutes while she's at work. *I appreciate the help; well she did this to me anyway. Out there carrying on with her ghetto self. She'll make a good girlfriend for some man one day.*

*****

I'll be glad when this court mess is over. With all these continuations, it's just holding me up. I completed my domestic violence, anger management and parenting classes that was ordered by the court. A bunch of nonsense. Anything so the state can collect some money. My Lawyer said I should just be looking at probation, but my restraining order will still be in effect. In order for me to see my kids it has to be supervised, like I'm some child beater. I'm still waiting for that to happen. The system is so slow. While I was at court I checked into filing for a divorce. I forgot we have to be separated for a year. I can't see myself ever getting married again; it's too hard to get out of it. Dominique must think I'm playing, but I'm so serious. I want a clean slate. The days of a woman tying me down are long gone.

I been saving my money up for my bachelor pad. This being out of work just set me back a couple of months. I want my own, where can't nobody put me out. I don't have to hear anyone's mouth yapping about this and that. Just straight up peace of mind. Be bothered when I feel like it.

*****

"Rich! Rich!" Keisha was yelling like she don't know I'm in this room.

"Yeah!" I yelled back. *She knows I can't just get up and run to her. She's so stupid sometimes.*

"Poncho is here to see you!" *Thank God I was getting house sick. Can't even hang with the squad.*

"I'm coming, give me a minute!" I grabbed my crutch and hopped out the room to the living room using my one good arm. I'm glad Keisha cleaned up this dirty house. It looks pretty good. Since I've been here I stay riding that ass. *She's going to do right as long as I have to be in here.*

*****

"My man," Poncho put his fist up. "You're getting there man. I had to come check on you."

"Yeah, I'm getting better. Staying higher than a mother fucker off these pills, not feeling no pain." *These pills are the truth. I see how people get addicted.*

Poncho laughed. "I hear that, so what's good?"

"Man, I feel like I'm about to lose my mind! Stuck like Chuck, can't do shit! The holidays coming up and I can't be mobile." *Just looking over there at Keisha pisses me off. It's almost time for her to go to work. I wish she would hurry up and go.*

"Yeah that's torture, but at least you're not locked up. It could be worse." Me and Poncho both glanced at Keisha. I can tell Poncho wants to talk about something but he can't say nothing in front of her.

*****

"Alright guys, I'm about to catch the bus to go to work. Boo, if you need anything just hit me up. I'll call to check on you later. Love you." Keisha tells me she loves me about fifty times a day. I think she's waiting for me to say it back, but my response is always the same, 'Uh huh' and a head nod. That's all I got for her. I used to fake it and tell chicks all the time that I loved them, now you can't pay me to say those three words. *Good, she finally went out the door to catch the bus. I'd let her take my car if she had her license.*

*****   .

"Man, I can't wait until I get right! I know my nieces and nephew been in that basement tearing shit up since I haven't been there." *Rob better be checking his kids, and all my stuff better be in there, or else he's paying for anything that they broke up.*

"Listen, that's the least of your worries. Shorty that you were dealing with is pregnant by you. She don't want you to know about the baby. Where did you find her at, and does she have any sisters that think like her? I could never be so lucky!" *Thanks for the bomb, Poncho. That, I could have done without.* Poncho is smiling, as usual, and I don't find a baby being funny, especially when I don't want any more.

"Come on man, you can't be serious! Where are you getting your info from? You are talking about Mika, right?" *Poncho got my head all fucked up. I need a drink and another pain pill.*

"Chris told me, and she's not lying. I heard the whole conversation. When Shorty found out that Chris was messing back with me she took ten steps back and part of the reason was because me and you are boys. She was worried that I would find out and tell you! Which is exactly what I'm doing now. I wouldn't even worry about it if I was you, just keep on acting like you don't know. Unless you want to bitch up and claim the baby!" Poncho reached out to give me a high five like shit was sweet. I just left him hanging. *Can't believe this fool.*

"Mika is lying. I'm not the father of that baby! What woman you know doesn't want her baby daddy in his, supposed to be child's life? I haven't been with her in months. She might be able to pull that off with her girls, but not me!" *I have to look into this so-called pregnancy. Mika didn't seem like the type to sleep around, but neither did Dominique. You can never be too careful with these women.*

"She's six months, so the timeframe does add up, and she was pretty adamant about me not finding out. She sounded pretty paranoid on the phone. If the baby belonged to some other dude I don't think she would have a problem with saying that. You might as well face it, you have another load on the way!" *Only me. Why do I always have to suffer?*

This couch is so uncomfortable, feels like wire up underneath my ass. They say you get what you pay for, and Keisha didn't have to come out her pocket, courtesy of the state. "Six months? Wow! Since when did Chris become 'buddy buddy' with Mika?"

"Duh, since Chris and Liz became BFF's, they been rolling together. I had to let you know, even though I told Chris I wasn't going to say nothing to you." *Chris and Keisha are cool, and Chris didn't tell Keisha. These women are trifling. Chris is playing both sides of the fence.*

"I'll hit her up when I can get out of here and ask her what's going on?" *I'm never going raw dog again. Mika was supposed to be on birth control. Another damn baby that I don't want. I have to get fixed, this is ridiculous.*

"Alright, check it out. On another note, wifey is claiming that she's pregnant too, and so is Honesty. You ain't the only one fucked. I am too." *No he's not. It's not like he's going take care of them or even get a job. That's their problem, just like the rest of his baby mama's.*

"Damn, and I'm over here contemplating on getting fixed. You need it more than me! What's this going to be, twelve and thirteen?" I put my hand on my head.

"Yep, that's sounds about right. But I'm not getting fixed. They want to have them, let them go right on ahead. Wifey only did that to be smart. She don't want to pay me no alimony or sell that house. She was advised by her lawyer to get pregnant. Now ain't that some shit!" *Sure is. She was smart and you're the stupid one.*

"What now? I guess you won't be getting that divorce." *Now what's the plan, Poncho? He always has one.*

"I can't divorce her right now, until after this baby comes. She also hired a private investigator to track my whereabouts. She came at me with pics of me, Chris, and Jordan, and she has pics of me and Honesty. She will eat me up in court. Chris and Honesty think that I will be divorced soon. Both of them are planning weddings and I can't let neither one of them down! Man, get ready to be the best man again…in both weddings!" *I must be trippin off these pain pills, my hearing is a little off.*

CHAPTER 21

LIZ

I've been looking for a place for me and my girls to live.

Stuff between me and Tyson was getting worse by the second. He's being so mean and nasty towards me, mad because he thinks I chose my friends over him. I really didn't, he just wasn't about to control me. At first I was sleeping on the couch, until he started waking me up in the wee hours of the morning. Coming downstairs making noise and turning on lights just to aggravate me. After about a week of that I started sleeping in the room with the girls. I been staying gone, as much as I can, for the most part.

When I get off work I pull up and toot the horn for the girls to come out so we can leave. I rotate between Wanda's, Mika's, and my Mom's house. The more I stay out of his way; you would think the better for the both of us. Not him, he's very spiteful.

The other day he blocked me in and wouldn't move his truck so that I could leave. I ended up stuck in the house with his miserable ass until the next morning. I was so pissed off that I started crying. Now I make it my business not to pull in the driveway. Yesterday when I pulled up, some chick was outside parked in her car and he had the audacity to be out there talking to her, disrespecting me. Smiling and grinning all up in her face. I went all the way off on him and her. Now I'm kicking myself because that's the reaction that he wanted. I wish I could have just been strong enough to wink and smile. My feelings were still tied to him though. Before I knew it I lost my composure. Making a fool out of myself, while he was telling me to go in the house and mind my business. Even the chick was chuckling until I came at her with my fist swinging. Then she decided to pull off. Almost ran me over; guess it wasn't too funny.

Because I have love for him, you couldn't pay me to disrespect him in no way shape or form. Just from that incident, I now know where I stand with him. I asked my mother if I could move in with her for a little while. She really doesn't have the room, but she said she'd make room, once she found out what happened. Mom didn't want me anywhere where I or her granddaughters weren't wanted. I hate bringing family and friends in the relationship, but I couldn't hold it in anymore. Everyone but Chris knew we were having problems, but they didn't know to what extent. My fear is that we would be all in love again. I forgive him but my family and friends wouldn't. I've been down that road with Poncho and I didn't want to make the same mistake again.

*****

I took the day off to pack all of our stuff while Tyson is at work. *By the time he comes home I should be done. With the way I'm moving, I might be out of here within the hour.* I'm doing it all by myself, didn't want to inconvenience anyone the day before the holiday when everyone is cooking and doing their last minute shopping. I was going to move after Thanksgiving, but after that stunt he pulled, enough was enough.

He wasn't giving me my mail. I don't know where he's hiding it. When I ask him for it, he just ignores me. He bumps into me on purpose, making me stumble. He won't flush the toilet whether he pees, shits, or spits. He makes a mess in the kitchen and he won't clean up behind himself, knowing I have OCD. Some nights I would be up cleaning until one or two in the morning then have to jump up and be back up by six. He wasn't eating my food when I did cook, and he wouldn't let TJ eat either. They would eat out or he would come in the kitchen and cook for just him and his son. I wake up and all my leftover food is in the trash, even my lunch dish. This last month has been hell and I refuse to have me and my girls living on eggshells.

*****

I heard the door open. *Please let it be TJ coming home from school early. I really can't deal with Tyson, moving out it's painful enough. My heart can't take much more. All I want to do is get out of here in peace and quiet. I finally took a chance on love again and got my feelings hurt again. It was good while it was good, but I'll be damned if I want to take the bad. I'm used to being with a dog that would kiss my ass at the drop of a dime. Tyson is a whole horse of another color. He's verbally and mentally abusive! I'm hurt beyond words. To the point where it shows all over my face, no matter where I go or how much I try and smile.*

I hear the footsteps and immediately know that it's Tyson. Whatever I have in the room that we used to share, he can have it. Right now I'm making sure that I have all my girls' stuff. That's what's important to me. *I parked the U-Haul in the driveway so he should know what's going down.*

*****

"Oh, you're just going to leave without saying goodbye to me or my son! Now you on some sneaky shit!" Tyson walked up on me while I was in the girls' room packing.

"The way you been acting? Hell no you don't get a goodbye from me. I left something for TJ. He didn't do anything to me." I put a note under his pillow letting him know that I loved him and I was sorry about what happened between me and his father. He has my number and is welcome to call me at anytime.

"I let you and the girls come and stay here! It didn't have to be this way. You chose your sorry ass bitches over me!" *I'm sick of him calling my friends out of their name.*

"No I didn't, I chose not to be controlled by you. You wanted me to dispose of people that were in my life before you ever came along. Not a damn one of them so-called bitches did anything to disrespect my relationship with you, not even Chris, and you fucked her! Whatever they chose to do with their lives it's theirs to do! You were trying to change the person that I am! I had so-called friends that left me for dead because of a man and you know what happened? When that man left their asses and shit went sour, they all came looking me up! I swore on God's green Earth that I wouldn't become not near one of them! Trust me. You wanted me and my girls here, and I paid my way. There were no handouts! Don't stand here in my face and act like you did me a favor when we both helped each other!" *Thank goodness I'm almost finished in this room. and the way this conversation is going, whatever I don't get just won't be got.*

"You're mad at me because I wanted more for you? You don't need friendships that suck the life out of you!" *He just doesn't get it, or the point that I'm trying to make. Talking to Tyson is like talking to a brick wall. I am who I am and he can't accept me.*

"Don't tell me what you think I need! Here you go again with them control issues, you are not me and I am not you! I would never do to you the things that you did to me! You showed me your true colors this past month! I don't want no part of you! You're a mean and nasty human being! That's what the hell I don't need!" I grabbed a box and walked downstairs to load it up on the truck. Tyson was right behind me.

"Can we talk before you do this?" *Now he wants to talk, gotts to be kidding me.*

I turned around and looked him eye to eye. "You had all month to talk to me, instead you showed me. There is no need to talk, my mind's made up!" I walked out, loading my box on the truck.

When I turned around Tyson grabbed me, sitting me down inside the truck, hugging and holding me as if his life had depended on it. Three weeks ago I would have embraced him, but now all I have to give is numbness. Maybe in due time I will feel different, but right now, I have nothing. A person can do a lot of a damage in a short time.

"Tyson, the kids have a half a day today, and I want to be finished by the time I pick them up." *All this hugging on me is holding up my progress.*

"Okay, I'll help you." Tyson sounded like a lost puppy.

He helped me gather up all the rest of my belongings, put everything in boxes and helped me load up the truck. Tyson apologized to me and I apologized to him. *If I hurt him in any way, that was never my intention. I just felt the importance of standing my ground.* I wished him a Happy Thanksgiving and he did the same. We both shed some tears, but ended on a good note and decided to stay friends, if that's even possible. *Maybe we did move too fast.* Who knows what the future might hold but for now, it's a wrap. It's a very sad day, but life keeps moving and so will I. I just wish he didn't take it so far. We didn't have to be in this space if he would have compromised, and if we both just talked it out. Two strong personalities and neither one of us wanted to bend.

CHAPTER 22

CHRIS

*W*ell it's Thanksgiving Day and I have put my foot in this food. Been up all night long cooking my behind off. I'm tired, but not sleepy, and excited all at the same time. Liz and the girls are coming over and Keisha, Rich and their kids. I'm sooped and ready for the festivities to begin. *I hope they're ready for an all nighter.* I have plenty of drinks and games for us to play. The living room is set up for the fellas to watch the football game while us ladies do us. I have the playroom all set up for the kids, and they have their own table in there.

*****

Poncho stepped out for a while. Nervousness set in down in the pit of my stomach. *He better be back here in time. I almost lost him for good because of my insecurities. I really let that fake wife of his get to me last week.*

Poncho wasn't answering my calls or returning any my texts for two days. I felt like I was losing my mind, couldn't sleep or eat. In the mornings I was getting up and running to the window every time a car drove past, just to see if it was him coming to get Jordan.

Finally, I said I wasn't going to live like this again, and rolled up on him at the spot. He's not hard to find, and that squad of his do the same thing every day; meet up at the same spot and hang out for a few hours. At first he was just standing there like he wasn't going to come over to the car to see what I wanted, but eventually he did. Jordan started jumping up and down in his carseat yelling, 'Daddy, Daddy', he was so excited to see his father. Poncho started playing with him from outside the window and then Jordan put his arms out for Poncho to grab him. Poncho opened the door, unbuckled Jordan and took him over to say hi and give the squad high fives. At this point Poncho still hadn't said one word to me. Then I saw when Rich took Jordan into the gas station with him and that's when Poncho walked over to the car and grabbed the carseat. He told me he would be dropping off Jordan in a few. I hauled ass to the house. It was a mess.

I hadn't done any cleaning or cooking since my little episode. I straightened up real quick, trying to put everything in order before they came back. When they got there, Poncho was just going to drop Jordan off and keep on going. I wasn't having it. Once again I apologized to him and damn near begged for him to forgive me. *I was so wrong for even coming at him like that, with all that rage I had inside of me. Sometimes I don't think, just reacting, and it's not always good.*

Jordan was even giving me grief about running his dad away. We talked for a long time. Poncho said this is my last chance. If I ever do that to him again, it's over and he means it! I'm putting my best foot forward, the last thing I want him to do is leave me after we've come this far. I love him like I just met him yesterday, and I can't wait to call him my husband and expand our family with another kid or two. *Unlike Lisa; running around lying to me about being pregnant.*

She knew exactly what buttons to push. Next time I see her, she's getting fucked up on sight! I swear I didn't think my hatred for her could get any stronger. All I want to do is bash her head in the cement. I'm patiently waiting. The divorce will be final soon, and the day that happens is the day she will have to deal with me. *That chick almost cost me everything!* I'm still treading on thin ice. I can see it in Poncho's eyes.

*****

That same day, while we were talking, we went to Zales to go get my ring, but the credit card declined. Lisa had cut him off. Guess she said she wasn't paying for no ring. It was all good. I got approved for a charge account and put it on that.

I get to show off my rock today and let the ladies know for sure that this wedding is going down. After we eat and everybody gets settled I'll probably throw in some wedding talk. I have everything planned out in my head. I just need to fill them in on my ideas. This week I'll be concentrating on getting a hall. I want to do an all in one since I don't belong to a church.

*****

Even though me and Mika are on speaking terms now I still haven't told her that I'm getting married, although I know Liz has told her by now. I'm not going to ask her to be in it because of the situation between her and Keisha. I think it would be kind of putting her in an awkward situation. On top of that, Rich is Poncho's best man and he's the last person she wants to see. I will just leave the invitation open for her to make a choice. From our conversation that we had she will most likely decline. She's worried about Rich finding out about the baby. Asking me why am I with Poncho after all he put me through? Why did I do Liz the way I did? I felt like I was on the stand and she was the prosecutor, homegirl was coming at me hard! I'm still trying to figure out what any of this had to do with her being mad at me. If I wanted to tell Rich about the baby then I would have, the moment I found out. It ain't my business so I'm staying out of it, plus Rich didn't tell me when Poncho was getting married. Payback is a bitch. As far as me and Liz, I just explained that to me, it was hard for me after all that I have been through with Poncho, and we all know that Liz is not a fan of his. I had to let her know that my bond with Poncho is not for anyone to figure out. That's my business and my choice. All that explaining was getting on my nerves. Anybody else I would have cussed out, but I took into consideration that she's pregnant. Her emotions are on a high and me and Liz are her only support.

*****

Now my mother just texted me letting me know that her and my sisters are coming. She wants to know what time is dinner? *Who does that the day of? This is some bullshit. I can't have them all over here. My whole mood just changed…now I'm stressed. I really just wanted to enjoy a peaceful Thanksgiving.* Her nor my sisters like Poncho. She can't stand Liz because of our past.

Mom has a smartass mouth that won't quit, but under no circumstances will I allow anyone to disrespect her. I'm literally trying to figure out how I'm going to pull this off. I could tell them to come at six or seven, that way we would have already eaten. *I don't know what to do. Let me see if I get in touch with Poncho and see what he says before I reply with a lie. Nope, I'm not calling him to give him a reason to not show up. I'm going to call her and get some things straight.*

*****

"Hello Mom, Happy Thanksgiving." I turned around and saw Jordan jumping up and down on the brand new couch that Poncho put on one of Lisa's charge cards a couple of months ago. *When I get off this phone he's going to get a beating. He knows better than that.*

"Thank you, same to you! Did you get my text?" Mom asked, sounding like she was in a good mood today.

"Yes, I invited you over a month ago and you said no!" *I want to know why the sudden change? Is she for real or is she trying to sabotage my plans?*

"Yeah well, I changed my mind. I see you're going the extra mile, so I might as well try. We're family and it's the holiday. We all belong together, enjoying each other. Let's just stop all of this distance!" *My mother is giving me credit for something. I'm not sure if I should pass out now or later. All of a sudden she cares about family. My sisters are like her puppets; whatever she says goes. I'm the only one that ever stood up for myself. She couldn't pull me away from Poncho by the snap of her little finger.*

"I already invited people that you don't really care for. I want to make sure that there isn't going to be any drama over here, especially with the kids around." *Not that any of this mattered to her. She wouldn't care if God was around. Like she always told me, 'Kids don't know nothing.'*

"I'm your mother, I don't give a damn who you invited! They better act right. I'm bringing some rice pudding and stuffed peppers. We're getting everything together now and will be over there shortly!" My mother hung up the phone. *No mother, you better act right!*

Great, I wonder if should uninvite Liz and the girls real quick. I'm sure her family is doing something and she just opted out to chill with me. No I can't do that. Poncho was excited about spending the holiday with at least four of his kids. The only thing left for me to do is to get on my knees and pray to the Lord up above. The tension that will be felt in here will cut like a knife. All this food with no appetites. They better eat up this food.

*****

As promised my mother arrived with my sisters, nieces, and nephews. I faked a smile even though I really felt like crying. My mother went and took over my kitchen, tasting everything and doctoring up what she thought didn't have enough flavor for her; messing up my whole feast for the evening. My sisters were stretched out on the couch looking at some reality show when the TV was supposed to be on the football game. I was left yelling at the kids who were doing whatever the hell they felt like because their mothers were glued to the TV, not watching them at all. Then I see my mother drinking glass after glass of my Sangria that was supposed to be for me, Keisha, and Liz.

*****

Keisha, Rich, and the kids arrived first. I was relieved that Rich was here before Poncho. This way he would have someone to talk to, just to make him feel more comfortable around my family. Everyone spoke and my mom was actually quite pleasant. Now I can't say that Liz will get the same treatment, but for now things are as good as can be expected.

*****

Poncho walked in and got the evil eye from my family, of course. *This is just as much his place as it is mine.* I greeted him with a warm hug and kiss. I was so relieved just to see him. And he showed up on time, as he promised. His facial expression was kind of shocked, so I nodded my head in a way letting him know that this was unexpected. I'm pretty confident that he caught my drift. He took Rich into the bedroom, which was good because Rich was still having a hard time getting around. This way Rich could relax on the bed. Those two were in there watching the game, going back and forth talking shit and getting loud. We could hear them from the other room. I smiled on the inside; glad he was at least having fun with his boy, but pissed off at my mom and sisters for not speaking to the man of my house.

Then Liz came in with Wanda and the girls and got the same reaction as Poncho did from my family. I had no idea that Wanda was coming and she wasn't invited, but oh well. Keisha cut her eye at me when she saw Liz, but greeted Wanda with open arms. *To my knowledge Liz has never done shit to Keisha, so why be hostile towards her? Everyone needs to let bygones be bygones and get over the pettiness.*

Poncho heard his girls so he came out the room and greeted them all with a big hug and kiss. Then he grabbed Liz and gave her a friendly hug, which I thought was a nice gesture. I heard my mother fake cough and mumble under her breath. Liz said hello to everybody, but they all gave her the cold shoulder, except me. My sisters rolled their eyes and my mother acted like she didn't hear her and Keisha. Just plain ole ignored her and started chatting it up with Wanda.

I want my mother and sisters gone. Keisha can follow if she doesn't straighten up! They are the problem and I shouldn't be feeling this way in my own place. I walked in the kitchen to greet the ringleader.

*****

"Mom, Poncho came in and you didn't speak to him, when he lives here. Liz spoke to you also and you didn't speak." *I've had enough already. The disrespect was at an all time high.*

My mother turned around and looked at me like I was the one in the wrong. "You say he lives here, I say he lives off of you, so any man like that doesn't deserve a hello from me! And that girl is your enemy, not your friend."

"Mom, Poncho paid for most of this stuff in here. What are you talking about? Don't you see this ring on my finger? You will respect the man of this house or you can leave! Everyone in here is welcome in this house. I really don't want the confusion. That's why I asked you before you even came over here!" I was trying to keep it down, not wanting to make the situation even more awkward than it already was.

"He didn't pay for shit, some woman did! But I'm not going to knock it, whatever the hustle is, is better than it coming out my daughter's pockets. Where is he? Let me go and apologize to my future son in law." My mother was walking her tipsy ass into my bedroom and I followed right behind her. "Hey gentleman, don't mean to interrupt, but dinner is ready and we're all about to eat at the dinner table. Chris cooked up all of this food for us, and I want us to eat as a family." Mom turned around and starting walking back towards the kitchen.

*****

"Yo, what was that?" Poncho asked, looking suspicious. "What did your mother cook? I need to make sure I don't eat any of it. " *He's right, I'm not eating them stuffed peppers or that rice pudding. For all we know, she might have some poison in it. That was not an apology.*

"You know what I cooked, just eat what you had on the menu! I'm going back in this kitchen to keep a close eye out!" Rich and Poncho started grinning, ready to bust out laughing, but I was dead ass serious. *This woman was on one.*

*****

I made my way back into the kitchen with my mother to help her prepare the plates, more like watch and make sure she wasn't up to no good. We got all the kids together first and made their plates, which was a job in itself, but lots of fun. Once we had them settled down at their table it was time for the grown folks to eat, all at the same table. The part that I was dreading.

174

We put most of the food in bowls, so that the adults can fix their own plates. Everyone sat down, passing the bowls around, filling up their plates, being nice and polite to one another. Poncho said the prayer and we all began to eat. *My mother didn't doctor up my food too much. It was still good. Well she can cook anyway.* It's just annoying when someone goes behind you, adding their ingredients into food that you cooked. That's just how she is though, walk in anybody's house and take over.

*****

"Wanda, I saw Champ the other day. He came in McDonalds to get something to eat. What happened?" Keisha asked. *I want to know myself. Ears are wide open.*

"Girl, he was messing with this chick Honesty for the past two years. She can have him. I'm good. Next subject!" *Well damn, poor Wanda. She was waiting on that man for years. Why is Poncho over there choking?*

"Sweetie, you okay?" I asked Poncho.

"Yeah, I'm good. The food just got stuck in my throat." Poncho got up to get some water.

"Well, I guess that taught you a nice long lesson. Never wait on any man! Keep it moving!" *My mother just had to chime in.*

"Keisha, how is your court case going with that chick you were fighting over Rich for?" *Oh no, the shade. Not today ladies. Now Wanda was coming back at Keisha. Rich looked like he wanted to piss on himself.*

"I'm good, just looking at some more probation time whenever we do go back to court. We straight over here, can't you see!" Keisha pointed at Rich. I glanced over at Liz, who was just enjoying her food, minding her business.

"Okay, I was just checking because I saw homegirl the other day. Just wanted to make sure you didn't try to do nothing to her or that baby she's carrying." *Shit! Fuck! Why, Wanda? Why?*

"What baby?" Keisha jumped up from the table, glaring down at Wanda.

"You better sit your ass down somewhere. I'm not her, Keisha! Yep, she's good and pregnant. I thought you knew! Rich didn't tell you? I thought you just said that y'all was good over there!" Wanda snapped her fingers. *Misery loves company and Wanda is coming for Keisha. Why did Keisha even feel the need to bring up Champ? They better take this outside.*

"Richard, is that bitch pregnant by you?" Keisha asked. She caught Rich off guard. He wouldn't answer her. "Since you can't answer me, I'll go ask her myself!"

"Oh no the hell you won't!" Liz jumped up.

A Thanksgiving From Hell!
To be continued...

OTHER BOOKS BY STACEY FENNER

A TOXIC LOVE AFFAIR
Available at: Amazon

Tyrone and Daniel are two best friends but total opposites. Tyrone has his woman at home taking care of the kids while he's out playing in the streets. He soon finds out that being too comfortable and secure will cost him everything when he comes home to an empty home.

Will his womanizing ways wreck his life or can he get it together before it's to late?

Daniel on the other hand, is still trying to heal from a messy divorce with Candace five years later. He's tried dating but finds it hard to move on.

Find out what happens with a good-looking man who has money to buy everything but is unfulfilled on the inside. A Toxic Love Affiar is filled with love, lust, hate and drama.

*****

A TOXIC LOVE AFFAIR 2
Available at: Amazon

They say once a good girl is gone she's gone forever, and if you thought Part 1 threw you for a loop, then get ready to do figure 8's this go around.

Belinda sets out on a mission to destroy all her childhood, so-called, friends that have betrayed her. She has no boundaries or limits to her destruction. She has intentions on making each and every one of them pay, and has masterminded a plan that will eventually cause her to self-destruct in the worst way!

Being disloyal to Belinda will cost them everything. Everybody likes to play but nobody wants to pay!

Meanwhile, Daniel finally opens himself up to love again after going through his messy divorce with his scandalous ex-wife, Candace. That won't last too long when a jealous Candace gets wind of the relationship; she throws a monkey wrench trying to exhaust him of all hope. Meanwhile, Daniel is stuck cleaning up the mess Tyrone created.

Find out if Tyrone and Daniel's friendship can survive the aftermath when Daniel gets wind to what Belinda is up to and he feels responsible for her trifling ways. Shocked is an understatement as to how he feels about a woman he once had so much respect for.

*****

A TOXIC LOVE AFFAIR 3
Available at: Amazon

These toxic relationships will take it to another level of trifling in this final installment of the Toxic Love Series.

Tyrone takes a trip back down memory lane and reunites with his drug-addicted mother on a quest to find out who his father is. After hooking up with Dana, Daniel's sister, Tyrone decides to turn in his player card and be a father to all of the children that he has fathered, but karma has a funny way of landing right back in his lap. Getting what he gave in life; will trouble from the past overcome him?

Daniel relocates back to Atlanta to be with Shaunda, the woman that he plans on spending the rest of his life with, but an unexpected visitor will come along and be the interruption of everything. Meanwhile, Shaunda reveals another side of herself that has Daniel questioning her pure existence. As Daniel's hatred toward his ex-best friend, Mr. Tyrone himself, grows after he learns of the secret relationship of Tyrone and Dana.

Sheree and Calvin's marriage is on the rocks once again because of Sheree's obsession in finding Belinda to seek revenge. Sheree bites off more than she can handle when another secret of hers is revealed.

Belinda makes her way back to the states and right back into the arms of her protector, Troy. But of course not without a twist to her madness.

Rivals will come face to face when a funeral places everyone in the same location...but who will meet their untimely demise?

*****

THE COMMANDMENTS OF A FEMALE HUSTLER
Available at: Amazon

Meet the well-known trio, Lala, Binky and Jay, who been rocking and rolling together since their childhood days. Raised in the projects these three had only one thing on their minds, the come up! These ladies will show you how to use what you got to get what you want!

What starts out as 'may the best woman win' ends in a rage of jealousy, dividing the three. After such a betrayal, can their relationship be fixed? What happens when the commandments are no longer followed? One will find love, one will end up behind bars, and one's mind is sick and twisted!

Swift, Jock, and Moose have the east side of Baltimore locked down with the drug game, but stuff gets twisted when there's a murder involved. When relationships fail, sex, lies and love take over. Their loyalty towards one another will be tested in the worst way. Rivals will meet, love will be found and hearts will be changed as the hustler game is taken to a whole new level of disrespect!

Who will be the sell out?

*****

THE COMMANDMENTS OF A FEMALE HUSTLER 2
Available at: Amazon

The worst thing a woman can do is bank on her looks. Lala will soon find out that beauty is only skin deep in the worst way! When you're a woman with no substance that carries a torch around filled with nothing but attitude, people tend to turn on you and you become as ugly as you are on the inside!

With Swift, Rock, and Sweets locked up in Chesapeake Detention Center, facing hundreds of years, Moose assumes the role of *Head Man in Charge*. Letting all the power go to his head, treating Lala like his intern, these two will clash, as they both suffer from control issues.

Jay's dream relationship with Boss is crashing down around her. The duo had it all, but as he goes downhill, he takes Jay right along for the ride! Stuck with three kids that don't belong to her, and taking care of her Grandmother, money is tight, leaving her no other choice but to go back to her old ways!

Running from Baltimore, with goals in mind of her and Jay living out their dreams of owning their own shop, Binky moves in with Jay to start her life over. Her love life takes off, headed in the right direction, but bad decisions will be her downfall, leaving her devastated and distraught!

Tighten your seatbelt and get ready for these twists and turns!

*****

NEW HAVEN RATCHET BUSINESS
Available at: Amazon

There's a lot that goes on in the small city of New Haven. Where the men have it their way, and prey on a woman's weaknesses!

Let me introduce you to the Bum Squad, which consists of Poncho, the ringleader, Rich, Quan, Mickey and Trey! Ladies, stay away from these types of men! Bums they are. They don't work, but manage to have all their needs and wants supplied by the women that they choose to date! These five men have it all with nothing to give!

Poncho is the dirtiest of them all, reeling women in, only to suck the life out of them, leaving them broken-hearted and confused! Rich, the washed up has-been finds himself stuck in a family affair that will have two cousins at each other's throats! Quan, Mickey, and Trey seem to understand their lane. They're not looking for much, just a place to lay their heads!

Liz and Chris are archenemies, both having a history with the infamous Poncho! Poncho does Chris in, leaving her suicidal and bitter! Liz runs to the rescue to dig her out of the pit of hell that she's mentally in!

Dominique and Keisha will face off over Rich and his lies of deceit. A gullible Mika will find herself involved in the trifecta love affair, as she becomes victim to Rich and his lies!

Find out what happens in the Ratchet New Haven Business.

About Stacey Fenner

Instagram: authorstaceyfenner
Twitter: sfenner1
Facebook: www.facebook.com/authorstaceyfenner

You can contact Stacey Fenner at
authorstaceyfenner@gmail.com

Stacey Fenner, was born December 1 and raised in New Haven, CT., the youngest of three. In 1999 Stacey relocated to Atlanta, GA where she resided for a year before moving to Baltimore, MD to care for her parents with her two daughters.

Writing since she was a child was a way to express herself, allowing her to overcome many trials and tribulations. However, she never pursued her gift until 2008. Although she obtained her degree in accounting, and currently works in that field, her passion is and always has been writing.

Stacey's writing career is focused upon novels about relationships. Her first book, A Toxic Love Affair, which was published in April of 2015, landed her in the #37 spot on the Woman's Urban Best Selling list. Her follow-up novel, A Toxic Love Affair Part 2, landed in the # 24 spot on that very same list. Having just recently finished up Part 3 of that series, Stacey is taking the Indie world by storm.

Made in the USA
San Bernardino, CA
10 March 2018